EATALY

ALL ABOUT

PASTA

A Complete Guide with Recipes

PIEMONTE
agnolotti del plin

VALLE D'AOSTA
pizzoccheri

LOMBARDIA
ravioli di zucca

TRENTINO—ALTO ADIGE
canederli

VENETO
bigoli

FRIULI—VENEZIA GUILIA
cialzon

EMILIA—ROMAGNA
cappelletti

LIGURIA
trofie

TOSCANA
pici

LE MARCHE
tagliatelle

UMBRIA
strangozzi

ABRUZZO
chitarrine

LAZIO
bucatini

MOLISE
malefante

CAMPANIA
paccheri

BASILICATA
maccheroni

PUGLIA
orecchiette

SARDEGNA
malloreddus

CALABRIA
filei

SICILIA
casarecce

EATALY

ALL ABOUT

PASTA

A Complete Guide with Recipes

WRITTEN WITH NATALIE DANFORD
PHOTOGRAPHS BY FRANCESCO SAPIENZA

RIZZOLI
NEW YORK

New York Paris London Milan

CONTENTS

PASTA SECCA 7

PASTA FRESCA 67

PASTA RIPIENA *135*

PASTA SECCA

Pasta makers fashion a world
out of water and flour.

LA PASTA DI GRAGNANO

THOUGH PASTA IS SIMPLE, NOT ALL PASTA IS CREATED EQUAL. The finest dried semolina pasta has long been made in the Campania region and specifically in the town of Gragnano, outside of Napoli, the birthplace of the modernized production of dried pasta. In 1842, King Ferdinand II, a Bourbon, was apparently so taken with the pasta he ate in Gragnano that he commissioned the town's pasta makers to provide for his royal court.

Dried pasta made with water and semolina flour is unquestionably one of man's greatest culinary inventions. A true "convenience food," it can be stored for months, it is relatively inexpensive, it cooks quickly, and it is filling and satisfying. It is also extremely versatile. Not only is dried pasta available in an uncountable number of shapes and sizes, but it pairs well with almost anything. You can enjoy pasta with fish, poultry, meat, vegetables, or dairy, and even *pasta in bianco*—prepared with just a generous dousing of olive oil and perhaps a sprinkling of grated cheese—makes a satisfying meal.

At Eataly, we sell dried pasta that is made in Gragnano using bronze molds. These molds create a microscopically rough surface that grips sauce; lesser-quality pasta is made in Teflon molds that create a perfectly smooth surface. Also, the pasta we sell is slow-dried at controlled temperatures; lesser-quality pasta is sometimes rushed with heating elements or fans. It can take as long as two days for pasta to dry naturally, but we think you'll agree that it's worth the wait.

➤ Dried semolina pasta from Italy is almost always sold in 500-gram packages, a little more than 1 pound. (Some Italian pasta is packaged for the United States in 1-pound packages, which weigh 454 grams.) This amount is perfect for serving four to six people as a *primo*, or first course.

UNA STORIA LUNGA

No one has ever successfully completed a survey of all the pasta shapes in the world. There are too many different shapes and multiple names for each. But those of us who have dedicated our lives to pasta do have ways of differentiating them from one another. One such division is to look at long and short pasta. As a basic rule, long dried semolina pasta pairs with oil-based sauces, smooth tomato sauces, and seafood.

When you cook long pasta, simply place it in the boiling water vertically and let it splay out. After a few seconds the part of the pasta that is submerged in the water will soften. Gently press with a wooden spoon to fold the pasta so that it is all submerged. Stir frequently (a long fork is useful) to keep the strands from sticking.

LINGUINE

"Little tongues" make a classic pairing with clams.
Unlike spaghetti, which are round, linguine are flat.

FUSILLI LUNGHI

These long twists of dried pasta capture
little bits and pieces in their coils. They look
like old-fashioned telephone cords.

BUCATINI

*Bucatini are long, thick strands of pasta with a
hole down the middle. ("Buco" means hole.)*

TONNARELLI

*Tonnarelli are similar in shape to spaghetti alla
chitarra (see page 93). From the Lazio region,
they are square if viewed from the short end.
They are often used in cacio e pepe (page 19).*

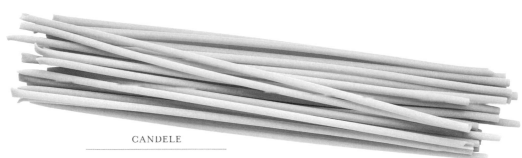

CANDELE

*Candele, "candles," resemble tapers.
They are thicker and wider than
bucatini and are often extra long.*

SPAGHETTI AL POMODORO
SPAGHETTI WITH TOMATO SAUCE

Serves 4 as a first course

If in a culinary Rorschach test someone said the words "Italian food" to you and then asked what image sprang to mind, you would likely be picturing a bowl of spaghetti with tomato sauce. This is perhaps the most famous Italian dish. It is not only simple and delicious, but can be made with ingredients that you probably have on hand most of the time. The quality of the tomatoes is front and center here, so it really matters—use only Italian tomatoes that truly taste of the Mediterranean sun. When finished, the tomato sauce should be a rich red color. If it is brick red, it's too thick and needs to be thinned with water.

¼ cup extra virgin olive oil, plus more for finishing

2 cloves garlic

1 pinch crushed red pepper flakes (optional)

1 (16-ounce) can whole peeled tomatoes in their juices

Fine sea salt to taste

3 to 4 sprigs fresh basil

Coarse sea salt for pasta cooking water

1 pound spaghetti

HEAT the olive oil in a large saucepan over medium heat. Crush the garlic cloves with the heel of your hand and discard skins. Add the crushed cloves to the oil and cook, stirring occasionally, until the garlic is golden brown, about 5 minutes.

ONCE the garlic is brown, add the red pepper flakes, if using, and then immediately add the tomatoes, crushing them between your fingers and letting them fall into the saucepan. Add the tomato juices as well. Season with salt to taste.

SIMMER the tomato sauce over low heat until slightly thickened, about 20 minutes. Add the basil sprigs to the sauce and set aside.

BRING a large pot of water to a boil for cooking the pasta. When the water is boiling, salt the water (see page 22), add the spaghetti, and cook, stirring frequently with a long-handled fork, until al dente. (See page 10 for more detailed instructions on the proper cooking technique for long dried pasta such as spaghetti.) Drain in a colander. If the tomato sauce has cooled completely, heat it gently.

REMOVE the basil sprigs from the tomato sauce and discard. Transfer the spaghetti from the colander to the pan. Toss over medium heat to combine. Add a drizzle of olive oil and serve immediately.

ALL FOR ONE AND ONE FOR ALL

COOKING PASTA IS PRETTY SIMPLE, but it almost always requires dirtying at least two pots: one for cooking the pasta in boiling water (see page 22) and one for preparing the sauce. There are, however, some pasta dishes that maximize efficiency (and minimize cleanup) by cooking pasta together with the other ingredients in the dish.

Soup, obviously, is one convenient possibility. See pages 72, 75, 154, and 163 for broth soups with fresh pasta, and page 59 for our favorite minestrone.

Pasta and bean dishes are often cooked together into a thick dish that is halfway between a soup and a stew. Soak dried beans (or shell fresh beans), then sauté a yellow onion in olive oil until golden and add the beans. Sauté for a few minutes, then add water to cover. When the beans are soft (al dente beans are an abomination in Italy), season with salt and stir in small pasta or broken spaghetti (the only time breaking spaghetti is appropriate) and simmer until the pasta is cooked through. Drizzle with a little more olive oil and serve. You can also puree the beans in the pot with an immersion blender before adding the pasta.

If you prefer, use canned beans (chickpeas are our choice), then cook the pasta risotto-style: Sauté minced yellow onion in extra virgin olive oil in a large skillet. Drain a can of chickpeas and add to the skillet. Sauté briefly, then with a fork roughly mash about two-thirds of the beans. Stir in small pasta, such as ditalini, and toss to combine, then add enough hot water just to cover the beans and pasta. Season with salt and cook, stirring, over medium-low heat until the water has been absorbed. Continue to add water in small amounts, stirring to combine between additions, until the pasta is tender. Season with a generous sprinkling of freshly ground black pepper and an equally generous drizzle of olive oil.

IL POTERE DEL GUSTO

Punchy, savory, umami—no matter how you say it, there are certain ingredients that form the flavor foundation of a dish. Visually they may fade into the background or even dissolve completely, but their flavor still gives an electric zing to every bite. Many of these "secret" ingredients are easy enough to keep in your pantry; keep them on hand and you will always have a winning pasta sauce at the ready.

OLIVE

The fruit of a tree, olives must be cured and/or fermented before they are ready to eat. Always a bit salty, they range from bitter to sweet. Green and black olives are the same fruit—green olives are not allowed to ripen before being picked.

SALE MARINO

In Italy, we cook with sea salt—fine sea salt for flavoring food and coarse sea salt for seasoning pasta cooking water. The salt pans in Trapani, Sicilia, are an excellent source for flavorful salt.

BOTTARGA

Bottarga is pressed fish roe. Mullet bottarga comes from Sardegna and Toscana; Sicilia and Calabria give us tuna bottarga. Purchase bottarga in whole chunks and grate it on a small-holed grater. Bottarga has an outer membrane that needs to be folded back before grating.

COLATURA

Colatura is an amber liquid made from fermented anchovies, a descendant of the garum of ancient Roma and a cousin to the fish sauce of southeast Asia. It comes from Cetara in Campania and is made from anchovies fished in the Gulf of Salerno in the period from March to July. The anchovies are cleaned, salted, and layered in wooden tubs. After several months, the liquid begins to drip through small holes in the tubs. It is very powerful.

POMODORI SECCHI

The best dried tomatoes are dehydrated slowly in the sun, usually spread on mats made of a natural material such as reeds. They are traditional in the south of Italy. They can be softened in hot water or soaked in olive oil until they are flexible.

ACCIUGHE SOTTO SALE

Whole anchovies preserved in salt are an Italian delicacy. Before using, rinse them off and debone them. Anchovies are usually roughly chopped and then dissolved further while cooking.

15

SPAGHETTI CON LA BOTTARGA
SPAGHETTI WITH BOTTARGA

Serves 4 as a first course

This is yet another recipe that is more than the sum of its simple parts, as the highest-quality ingredients are required. Always purchase bottarga—pressed fish roe—in a whole piece and grate it yourself for best results. You may use either tuna bottarga or mullet bottarga. Mullet bottarga has a more mild flavor; it hails from Sardegna and the coast of Toscana. Tuna bottarga, which is more assertive and darker in color, is native to Sicilia and parts of Calabria. Bottarga will keep for about one year in the refrigerator after its vacuum packaging is opened (or its beeswax coating is removed). It has an outer membrane that needs to be removed before grating—simply peel back the membrane of the size chunk you think you'll need and leave the rest covered.

¼ cup extra virgin olive oil

1 clove garlic

¼ teaspoon crushed red pepper flakes (optional)

½ cup fine breadcrumbs (see page 87)

2 tablespoons grated bottarga

Coarse sea salt for pasta cooking water

1 pound spaghetti

¼ cup minced fresh parsley

BRING a large pot of water to a boil.

HEAT the olive oil in a large pan over medium-low heat. Add the garlic and red pepper flakes, if using, and cook, stirring frequently, until the garlic is golden. Remove and discard the garlic. Add the breadcrumbs to the pan and cook, stirring constantly to keep them from burning, until they are golden, about 3 minutes. Remove from the heat. Stir in the bottarga.

MEANWHILE, once the water is boiling, add salt (see page 22 but keep in mind that the bottarga will be salty), and then add the spaghetti. Cook, stirring frequently with a long-handled fork, until spaghetti is al dente. (See page 10 for more on the proper cooking technique for long dried pasta.)

WHEN the pasta is cooked, reserve about 1 cup cooking water, then drain the pasta in a colander. Transfer the pasta to the pan with the breadcrumb mixture. Toss vigorously over medium heat until combined, about 2 minutes. If the pasta looks dry, add some of the cooking water, 1 to 2 tablespoons at a time, and toss between additions until the consistency is saucier. Garnish with the minced parsley and serve immediately.

BUCATINI CON LE SARDE
PASTA WITH SARDINES

Serves 4 as a first course

Hailing from Sicilia, this dish features a flavorful sauce made with fresh sardines, which is perfectly highlighted by the long hollow strands of bucatini. The traditional recipe calls for wild fennel, but cultivated fennel bulbs and greens are a good substitute.

3 pounds whole fresh sardines

Fine sea salt and freshly ground black pepper to taste

½ cup durum semolina flour

1 cup extra virgin olive oil

2 pounds fennel bulbs, greens removed and reserved, bulb cut into sticks

2 medium yellow onions, minced

3 tablespoons currants or raisins, soaked and drained

1 (28-ounce) can whole peeled tomatoes, drained and chopped

3 tablespoons pine nuts, lightly toasted

1 pinch saffron threads

Coarse sea salt for pasta cooking water

1 pound bucatini

REMOVE the heads of the sardines and gut and debone them. Set aside a few for garnish, then chop the rest. Season the sardines for garnish with salt and pepper and dredge them in the semolina flour. Heat ½ cup of the olive oil in a medium saucepan over medium heat. When the oil begins to smoke, brown the flour-coated sardines, about 1 minute per side. Remove the sardines from the pan with a slotted spatula and drain on a paper towel.

IN a large skillet, heat the remaining ½ cup olive oil and sauté the fennel bulbs until browned. Add the onions, currants, tomatoes, pine nuts, and saffron to the skillet and season with salt and pepper. Bring to a simmer, then add the chopped sardines and cook, stirring occasionally with a wooden spoon, until the sardines have broken down and are thoroughly mixed into the sauce, 10 to 15 minutes.

MEANWHILE, bring a large pot of water to a boil and season with coarse sea salt. Add the bucatini and cook until al dente (see page 22). (If the sauce in the skillet looks dry, thin it with a little of the pasta cooking water.) Drain the cooked pasta, transfer to a warm serving bowl, and add about three-quarters of the sauce. Stir to combine. Top the pasta with the remaining sauce and the fried sardines for garnish. Cover the pasta and let it rest for 2 minutes. Garnish with the reserved fennel fronds and serve immediately.

➤ Ask your Eataly fishmonger to fillet the sardines if you like.

SPAGHETTONI CACIO E PEPE
THICK SPAGHETTI WITH CRUSHED
BLACK PEPPER AND PECORINO

Serves 6 as a first course

Long pasta with grated cheese and a generous amount of cracked black pepper is a Roman signature. While it may seem simple, when made properly it is a truly memorable start to a meal.

2 tablespoons unsalted butter

2 tablespoons whole black peppercorns, or more to taste

Coarse sea salt for pasta cooking water

1 pound spaghettoni

1½ cups freshly grated Pecorino Romano, or more to taste

BRING a large pot of water to a boil.

HEAT the butter in a large saucepan over medium heat. Grind the peppercorns very coarsely and add them to the butter.

WARM up a large pasta serving bowl. (The easiest way to do this is to add some of the boiling water for the pasta and swish it around in the bowl, then discard it.)

WHEN the water is boiling, salt it (see page 22) and add the pasta. Cook until al dente (see page 22).

QUICKLY lift the pasta from the pot with tongs, letting it drain for an instant, then drop it directly into the saucepan. Mix the pasta with the sauce until well coated.

REMOVE the pan from the heat and immediately scatter 1 cup of the grated cheese over the pasta, tossing in quickly. As you mix, sprinkle over a spoonful of hot water from the cooking pot to moisten and unify the pasta and sauce. Taste and add more pepper and/or cheese as desired.

SERVE immediately, while the spaghettoni are very hot.

BUCATINI ALL'AMATRICIANA
BUCATINI WITH GUANCIALE

Serves 4 to 6 as a first course

Amatrice in northern Lazio is the source of this delicious pasta. After a 2016 earthquake devastated the town, Italian restaurants around the world—including Eataly's—donated funds from the sale of its legendary pasta dish to help rebuild.

¼ cup extra virgin olive oil

4 ounces guanciale, cut into ½-inch-wide strips

1 medium red onion, halved lengthwise and cut lengthwise into ¼-inch slices

¼ cup tomato paste

1½ to 2 teaspoons crushed red pepper flakes

¾ cup tomato puree, simmered until reduced by half

Fine sea salt to taste

Coarse sea salt for pasta cooking water

1 pound bucatini

1 cup freshly grated Parmigiano Reggiano or Grana Padano

⅓ cup coarsely chopped fresh flat-leaf parsley

BRING a large pot of water to a boil.

MEANWHILE, in a large skillet combine the oil, guanciale, and onion and cook over medium-high heat, stirring frequently, until the guanciale is lightly browned and the onion is softened, about 7 minutes. Stir in the tomato paste and red pepper flakes and cook, stirring, until fragrant, about 1 minute. Stir in the tomato puree and cook for 1 additional minute. Taste and adjust salt (you may not need any) and then remove from the heat.

SEASON the pasta cooking water with coarse salt and cook the pasta until just al dente (see page 22). Drain, reserving about ½ cup of the pasta water.

ADD the pasta and ¼ cup of the reserved pasta water to the guanciale and tomato sauce mixture in the skillet and stir and toss over medium heat until the pasta is well coated (add a splash or two of the reserved pasta water if necessary to loosen the sauce). Stir in about ½ cup of the cheese and the parsley and serve immediately, passing the remaining grated cheese on the side.

➤ A quick variation: omit tomato puree and paste to make pasta alla gricia.

HOW TO COOK PASTA

WE ITALIANS ARE RELAXED ABOUT A LOT OF THINGS, but cooking pasta is not one of them. Whether you are preparing dried, fresh, or stuffed pasta, you will follow the same basic steps every time.

Bring a large pot of water to a boil. There should be plenty of room for the pasta to circulate. Sometimes fresh pasta is cooked in batches to avoid crowding the pot. Use a lid to bring it to a boil more quickly.

Salt the water. Pasta cooked in unsalted water will never taste right—it absorbs the salt as it cooks. Pasta cooking water should be just slightly less salty than the sea. (If you are using salty ingredients, such as salted anchovies or capers in the sauce, keep that in mind for balance.) Take off the lid and add a handful of coarse sea salt to the boiling water. This may look like a lot, but most of the salt washes away when you drain the pasta.

After adding the salt, wait for the water to return to a boil, then add the pasta. As soon as you add the pasta, stir with a wooden spoon or long-handled fork. Do not break long pasta to fit it into the pot. Simply wait a moment for the pasta immersed in the water to soften, then push the remainder of the pasta into the water. Stir frequently while the pasta is cooking. Across Italy, cooks adding pasta to the water announce, "*Butto giù!*"—I'm throwing in!—which indicates a roughly ten-minute countdown until the meal will be served.

Cook pasta al dente. Fresh pasta is usually ready when it floats to the surface of the cooking water. Dried semolina pasta has a cooking time on the package. Start testing 1 to 2 minutes before the cooking time provided. There is no cure for overcooked pasta. To test dried semolina pasta, fish out one piece with a skimmer or fork and take a bite. If the center is still brittle and has a chalky white color, it's not ready. When it is al dente, there will be a slight resistance "to the tooth," but nothing hard, and the color will be mostly uniform throughout with just a slightly lighter color in the center. Like Riccioli d'Oro (you know her as Goldilocks), you're looking for something just right—not overcooked and not undercooked.

Drain the pasta. Either place a colander in the sink and pour the pasta and water into the colander, or use a slotted spoon or skimmer to remove the pasta from the pot. Transfer the pasta to a skillet or serving bowl. Often you will reserve some of the cooking water. Always turn off the burner as you remove the pot—never leave pasta sitting in its cooking water off the heat.

Finish and serve immediately. Pasta waits for no one.

BUCATINI AL TONNO
BUCATINI WITH TUNA

Serves 4 as a first course

Transport your kitchen to colorful Calabria with this recipe for pasta with tuna. Spiced with Calabrese chile peppers and brightened with capers, the seaside classic highlights the simple flavors of the southern region. Just back away from the grated cheese—we Italians never serve grated cheese on pasta with fish. Calabrese chile peppers are small red chile peppers similar to cayenne peppers that are sold preserved in olive oil.

2 tablespoons plus 1 teaspoon extra virgin olive oil

1 yellow onion, minced

1 clove garlic, sliced

1 Calabrese chile pepper in olive oil or fresh red chile pepper, drained and minced

1 (7-ounce) jar Italian tuna preserved in olive oil, drained

2 tablespoons salted capers, rinsed and drained

Zest of 1 lemon, grated

¼ cup breadcrumbs (see page 87)

Coarse sea salt for pasta cooking water

1 pound bucatini

BRING a large pot of water to a boil.

PLACE the 2 tablespoons olive oil in a large pan over medium-low heat. Add the onion, garlic, and chile pepper and cook, stirring frequently, until the onion and the garlic are golden. Flake the tuna into the pan and cook until tuna is heated through, about 2 minutes. Stir in the capers and the lemon zest and remove from the heat.

TOSS the breadcrumbs with the remaining teaspoon olive oil and toast in a toaster oven or in a cast-iron skillet over medium heat until crisp.

MEANWHILE, when the water in the large pot boils, add salt, and then add the bucatini. Cook, stirring frequently with a long-handled fork, until the bucatini is al dente. (See page 10 for more on the proper cooking technique for long dried pasta.)

WHEN the pasta is cooked, reserve about 1 cup cooking water, then drain the pasta in a colander. Transfer the pasta to the pan with the tuna. Toss vigorously over medium heat until combined, about 2 minutes. If the pasta looks dry, add some of the cooking water, 1 to 2 tablespoons at a time, and toss between additions until it looks moist. Garnish with the toasted breadcrumbs and serve immediately.

A Perfect Coat

You've boiled your water, salted it, cooked your pasta al dente, and drained it. So now what? Dried semolina pasta is a blank canvas for all kinds of ingredients. (Though there are some rules about matching pasta and sauce: see page 38.) Pasta cooks quickly, so you must have your sauce at least underway while it is in the pot. You don't want your pasta sitting in a colander and cooling off and clumping while something is reducing in a skillet. Use a restrained hand with sauce. The sauce should coat the pasta, but you should still be able to see the surface of the pasta underneath and taste the grain.

Remember our rant on page 8 about bronze dies? Well, the rough, pocked surface of the dried semolina pasta we serve at Eataly exists due to those bronze dies, and those teeny crags and indentations are the reason our pasta tastes so good. The sauce just doesn't coat the pasta—it soaks into it. The two become one.

There are two basic ways to combine the pasta and the sauce. You can either toss them together in a bowl, or you can toss them together in a skillet over heat. Tossing together in a bowl is the method to use for uncooked pasta sauces, such as pesto. But most cooked sauces will cling to the pasta more evenly if the two are tossed together over heat for a minute or two.

We always drain pasta, but the pasta doesn't become 100 percent dry, and the water that clings to it and the cooking water contain some of the starch from the pasta. (That's why the cooking water is cloudy, not clear.) As you cook pasta over the heat, the cooking water emulsifies with the sauce, makes it creamier, and gives it body. Always add cooking water in small amounts—a tablespoon or so at a time. There's nothing more unappetizing than a pool of water at the bottom of a bowl of pasta.

And don't go overboard with the skillet cooking. You can overcook pasta in the skillet just as easily as you can overcook it in the pot. A minute or two is all that's needed. Turn the heat to medium high, and *constantly* toss the pasta. Short pasta can be tossed with a spoon, but for long pasta you'll need tongs or two long-handled forks. If you're using two forks, hold them in one hand in a narrow V-shape. (Hold the skillet handle with the other hand—you don't want the pan flying off the stove!) Toss vigorously, pulling strands from the bottom of the skillet up to the top.

The pasta should still have moisture clinging to it when it is added to the pan with the sauce.

Use tongs to toss long pasta in the pan, being sure to coat every strand with sauce.

LINGUINE ALLE VONGOLE
LINGUINE WITH CLAMS

Serves 6 as a first course

This classic primo relies on excellent-quality clams, the smaller the better. Any of Campania's three white wine superstars—Greco Bianco, Fiano, Falanghina—would work well here.

3 tablespoons extra virgin olive oil, plus more for drizzling

4 cloves garlic, thinly sliced

2 pounds small clams, such as cockles, thoroughly cleaned

¼ cup white wine

Leaves of 4 sprigs fresh flat-leaf parsley

Coarse sea salt for pasta cooking water

1 pound linguine

Freshly ground black pepper to taste

HEAT the olive oil in a large sauté pan over medium heat. Add the garlic and cook, stirring frequently, until just beginning to color. Add the clams and then the wine. Cover the pan and turn the heat to high. Cook the clams just until they open, moving them with tongs to a bowl as they do. All of the clams should be open after about 5 minutes. Discard any unopened clams.

MEANWHILE, bring a large pot of water to a boil.

CHOP the parsley and add about half of it to the pan where the clams cooked. Remove some or all of the clams from their shells and return them to the pan, along with any liquid that collected in the bowl.

WHEN the water in the large pot boils, add salt (see page 22), and then add the linguine. Cook, stirring frequently with a long-handled fork, until the linguine is al dente. (See page 22.) Drain in a colander.

ADD the cooked linguine to the pan with the clams and toss vigorously over medium-high heat for 1 to 2 minutes. Sprinkle on the remaining parsley, season with pepper, drizzle with a little olive oil, and serve hot.

NOTE: To clean clams, place the clams in a bowl filled with plenty of cold water and a little salt. Let the clams soak for about 30 minutes. They should expel any sand contained in the shells. If any clams open, tap them gently; they should close readily. If not, discard them. With your hands, lift the clams out of the water and set them aside. Rinse the bowl, fill it with clean water, then soak the clams again for about 10 minutes. Repeat a third time, or until the water is free of sand. Scrub the clams against each other under running water to remove any grit from the shells. Rinse thoroughly.

LA PASTA TUBOLARE

Tube-shaped dried semolina pasta, with its hollow centers, is perfect for capturing ingredients. Match the sauce you are making with the diameter of the pasta's opening. Larger tubes such as calamari are perfect for bigger items, while smaller tubes such as penne pair well with peas and smaller diced ingredients.

Tubular pasta tends to cook fairly quickly. Taste early and often to be sure you catch it when it is perfectly al dente.

LUMACONI

These large snails are curved and hollow. They are large enough to be stuffed and baked (see page 166), and they also are delicious simply tossed with a sauce in a skillet. Lumachine are the tiny version of these, perfect for soup.

PACCHERI

Large-diameter paccheri are robust and stand up to chunky sauces. Legend has it that they were invented to smuggle contraband garlic across the Alps. The name is Neapolitan dialect for a slap, reportedly because as the large pieces of pasta hit the plate they sound like someone being slapped across the face. Paccheri may be tossed in a sauce, or they can be stuffed with a filling and baked.

MEZZE MANICHE

Perhaps because of their association with warm weather, mezze maniche, or "short sleeves," are often paired with uncooked sauces, such as chopped fresh tomatoes. Also known as maniche di frate, or "monk's sleeves," they are sturdy enough to be tossed vigorously in a skillet.

PENNE RIGATE

Penne, or quills, are probably the most versatile pasta there is and can be served with just about any sauce. Penne rigate are lined with ridges on the outside.

CALAMARI

Wide tubes of pasta do resemble the squid bodies that give them their name. They also match well with seafood sauces—a culinary pun of sorts.

RIGATONI AL CAVOLFIORE
RIGATONI WITH CAULIFLOWER

Serves 4 as a first course

In this fresh dish, cauliflower is highlighted by a surprise ingredient. Parsley and basil draw the lion's share of attention in the Italian herb garden, but mint should not be overlooked. It is especially intriguing here in combination with chile pepper.

1 head cauliflower

¼ cup extra virgin olive oil

1 large red onion, thinly sliced and cut into sticks

Fine sea salt to taste

3 salted anchovy fillets, rinsed, dried, and chopped

¼ cup sliced garlic

1 tablespoon crushed red pepper flakes

8 tablespoons (1 stick) unsalted butter, cut into pieces

½ cup pitted green olives, halved

Zest of 1 lemon in strips

Coarse sea salt for pasta cooking water

1 pound rigatoni

½ cup grated aged Pecorino cheese

Leaves of 1 small bunch fresh mint

BRING a large pot of water to a boil for the pasta. Meanwhile, cut the cauliflower into small florets and dice the stem.

IN a large skillet, heat the oil and add the red onion and diced cauliflower stems. Season with salt and sauté until softened, about 3 minutes. Add the anchovy fillets and garlic and sauté until the cauliflower begins to brown. Add cauliflower florets and sauté another 3 minutes. Add red pepper flakes and sauté for less than a minute, then add water just to cover. Lower heat and simmer until cauliflower is soft and liquid has reduced by two thirds. Stir in the butter, olives, and zest.

WHEN the water comes to a boil, season with coarse salt and cook the rigatoni until al dente. (See page 22.) Reserve a little pasta cooking water and drain pasta, then add to the skillet with the sauce. Toss over medium-high heat until combined, about 2 minutes, incorporating pasta cooking water if necessary. Sprinkle with grated cheese and mint and serve immediately.

➤ Cook the cauliflower in vegetable broth (page 74) rather than water for added flavor.

PASTA ALL'ARRABBIATA
PASTA IN SPICY TOMATO SAUCE

Serves 4 as a first course

Arrabbiata means "angry," but this dish always makes us pretty happy! The name references the hot pepper. You can, of course, increase the amount here if you have chile fans coming for dinner.

1 pound plum tomatoes, 6 to 8

¼ cup extra virgin olive oil

2 cloves garlic

½ teaspoon crushed red pepper flakes, or more to taste

Fine sea salt to taste

Coarse sea salt for pasta cooking water

1 pound dried semolina pasta, such as penne or other short tubular shape

1¼ cups grated Pecorino Romano

5 to 6 fresh basil leaves, torn

TO peel the tomatoes, cut an X in the bottom of each tomato. Bring a pot of water to a boil and with a slotted spoon or skimmer lower the tomatoes into the water. Boil until the skin begins to peel away where it was cut. Remove to a colander with the slotted spoon or skimmer and drain until cool enough to handle. Using a paring knife to lift the cut pieces of skin, peel the tomatoes over a bowl to collect the juices. (The skins should peel off easily.) With your hands, crush the tomatoes and reserve in the bowl with the juices. (See photos, opposite.)

HEAT the extra virgin olive oil in a skillet and sauté the garlic over medium-high heat. When the garlic is aromatic, remove from the pan and discard. Add the red pepper flakes and reduce the heat to low. Stir until fragrant, about 4 minutes. Add the crushed tomatoes. Simmer over medium heat, stirring occasionally, until the tomatoes have broken down and their juices have reduced but the pan is not entirely dry, about 8 minutes. Season to taste with fine sea salt.

MEANWHILE, bring a large pot of water to a boil and season with coarse salt. Add the pasta and cook until just al dente, about 2 minutes less than the package instructions. With a slotted spoon or skimmer, transfer the pasta to the skillet, reserving cooking water. Cook the pasta in the sauce, tossing, for 2 minutes. If the skillet looks dry, add a small amount of the cooking water to the pan. Top the pasta with grated cheese and basil and serve hot.

After a brief dip in boiling water, the skin should pull away from the tomato easily.

Your hands are the best tools for crushing tomatoes to use in sauce.

PACCHERI CON SUGO DI MARE
PACCHERI WITH SEAFOOD SAUCE

Serves 4 as a first course

Paccheri are wide tubes of pasta with lots of room for capturing bits of seafood in this tasty, savory sauce. Paccheri are also sometimes cooked and filled like cannelloni.

3 cups extra virgin olive oil, plus more for drizzling

Zest of 1 lemon in wide strips

8 ounces fresh tuna belly

Fine sea salt to taste

Freshly ground black pepper to taste

20 medium shrimp, shelled and deveined

20 mussels

½ cup dry white wine

Coarse sea salt for pasta cooking water

1 pound paccheri pasta

1 clove garlic

Pinch crushed red pepper flakes

½ cup tomato puree

2 tablespoons chopped fresh flat-leaf parsley

IN a small saucepan, combine the olive oil and strips of lemon zest. Place over low heat and, using a thermometer, bring the oil to about 130°F. Season the tuna with fine sea salt and pepper, add it to the saucepan, and poach the tuna in the oil until it is medium rare, about 7 minutes. Remove the tuna from the oil and set aside. Strain the oil and discard the lemon zest. Reserve the oil. (You won't use all of it in this recipe, but it can be used in other dishes.)

CHOP the shrimp into ¼-inch pieces. Thinly slice the poached tuna.

PLACE the mussels in a medium pot set over medium heat. Add the wine and cover with a tight-fitting lid. Remove the mussels from the pot as they open. Strain any liquid left in the bottom of the pot through a coffee filter or cheesecloth and set aside in a bowl. Remove the mussels from their shells and set aside in the bowl with the strained liquid.

BRING a large pot of water to a boil for the pasta. When the water is boiling, salt it (see page 22) and add the pasta. Cook until al dente (see page 22).

IN a large pan, heat about 3 tablespoons of the oil from poaching the tuna. Crush and peel the garlic clove and add it to the pan with the red pepper flakes. Sauté until the garlic is golden, then remove and discard the garlic. Add the tomato puree and cook until slightly reduced, about 5 minutes. Add the shrimp to the pan and toss until cooked, about 1 minute. Add the sliced tuna.

WHEN the pasta is cooked, drain it in a colander, then transfer it immediately to the pan with the seafood. Toss a few times, then add the mussels and their cooking liquid. Toss vigorously over medium heat until the pasta and seafood are combined, about 1 minute. Drizzle with a generous amount of olive oil, sprinkle on the parsley, and serve immediately.

Pasta Tombola

In Italy we play a game called *tombola*—it's a lot like bingo: one person calls out numbers and letters and you need to match those up on your chart. Far be it from us to suggest that pairing pasta is a game. It's an art that we take quite seriously! But you can use this *tombola* card to come up with some interesting combinations. No matter which way you look at it, that sounds like a win!

	SUCH AS…	LONG PASTA Fettuccine, Spaghetti, Tagliatelle	SHORT PASTA Paccheri, Penne, Vesuvio	STUFFED PASTA Cappelletti, Ravioli, Tortellini
CREAMY OR MEATY SAUCE	Amatriciana, Bolognese, Cacciatore	Tagliatelle alla Bolognese		
HEARTY AND CHUNKY SAUCE	Norma, Norcina, Ragù		Vesuvio con Scarola	
SIMPLE AND LIGHT SAUCE	Aglio e Olio, Butter and Sage, Pesto			Ravioli al Burro Fuso

PASTA ALLA NORCINA
PASTA WITH PORK SAUSAGE AND BLACK TRUFFLES

Serves 4 to 6 as a first course

Norcia is a town near Perugia famed for pork butchery and sausage making. To add luxury to this dish, end with a little of Umbria's *tartufo nero,* or black truffle.

½ cup extra virgin olive oil

1 clove garlic, peeled and crushed

½ pound sweet Italian sausage, casing removed, crumbled

3 tablespoons minced mushrooms

¼ cup white wine

⅓ cup heavy cream

Coarse sea salt for pasta cooking water

1 pound short tubular dried semolina pasta, such as penne

2 tablespoons unsalted butter

¼ cup grated Grana Padano cheese (see page 87)

¼ cup chopped fresh flat-leaf parsley

2 ounces fresh black truffle

BRING a large pot of water to a boil for the pasta.

MEANWHILE, in a skillet heat the oil and add the garlic. When the garlic begins to sizzle, add the sausage. Once the sausage has browned, add the mushrooms and cook, stirring frequently, until combined. Add the wine and simmer until the liquid has evaporated. Add the cream and stir to combine, then turn down the heat to a gentle simmer.

WHEN the water for the pasta is boiling, season with coarse salt and add the pasta. Add the butter and grated cheese to the skillet. Once the pasta is cooked al dente (see page 22), drain it, reserving about 1 cup cooking water, and transfer the pasta to the skillet with the sauce. Toss the pasta over medium-high heat until it is evenly incorporated into the sauce, about 2 minutes. Adjust for seasoning and add some pasta cooking water if the pan becomes too dry.

TRANSFER to a serving dish, top with parsley, and shave the truffle on top. Serve immediately.

GETTING OUT THE GLUTEN

GLUTEN IS A PROTEIN IN GRAINS, ESPECIALLY WHEAT. It is what makes flour bind together in a web. It is not unhealthy in and of itself, but people who have celiac disease and other dietary issues often have strong negative reactions to gluten. Interestingly, wheat allergies and gluten sensitivity are growing problems in Italy, too. As a result, we make a special effort to provide gluten-free options at Eataly, including pasta made with a mix of corn, quinoa, and rice flour; pasta made with lentil flour; and pasta made with ground chickpeas. Not a speck of gluten among them.

PASTA ALLA NORMA
PASTA WITH EGGPLANT

Serves 4 as a first course

Pasta alla Norma showcases Sicilia's flavorful eggplant, along with aged ricotta salata cheese. The name is an homage to the much-lauded opera *Norma* by Vincenzo Bellini, a native of Catania, Sicilia. Legend has it that upon tasting the dish in the 1800s, Sicilian playwright Nino Martoglio was so impressed that he compared it to the *bel canto* classic. You can fry the eggplant if you like, but we find it tastier when roasted, and it doesn't make a mess that way. Ricotta salata is ricotta that has been pressed, salted, and dried. We like to cut it into cubes for a pretty presentation, but if you'd rather, you can shred it and sprinkle it on.

2 medium eggplants (about 3 pounds total)

Fine sea salt to taste

2 tablespoons extra virgin olive oil

1 clove garlic, minced

1 medium red onion, diced

1 cup tomato puree

Coarse sea salt for pasta cooking water

1 pound penne or other short dried semolina pasta

5 ounces ricotta salata, cubed

Leaves of 1 sprig fresh basil

CUT the eggplants into ¾-inch cubes. Place in a colander, sprinkle with fine sea salt, and toss to combine, then set the colander over a bowl (or directly in a sink) and allow the eggplants to drain for 1 hour.

PREHEAT the oven to 350°F.

PAT the eggplant cubes dry and toss them with 1 tablespoon olive oil. Season with salt, keeping in mind that you've already salted the eggplant once. Spread the eggplant on a baking sheet (lined with foil for easy cleanup, if you like) and roast in the preheated oven for 15 minutes without disturbing. Turn the eggplant once—the undersides should be nicely browned, and continue roasting until the pieces are golden brown and soft, 15 to 20 minutes longer. Set the eggplant aside.

BRING a large pot of water to a boil for cooking the pasta.

IN a large skillet, heat the remaining tablespoon of olive oil over medium heat and add the garlic and onion. Cook until the onion is translucent and the garlic is fragrant, about 3 minutes, then add the tomato puree and season with salt. Decrease the heat and simmer until thickened, about 10 minutes.

MEANWHILE, when the water in the large pot boils, add coarse salt (see page 22) and then add the penne. Cook, stirring frequently with a wooden spoon, until the penne is al dente. (See page 22 for more on the proper cooking technique for dried pasta.)

WHEN the pasta is al dente, drain it in a colander. Add the eggplant to the skillet with the tomato and toss to combine, then transfer the drained pasta to the pan. Toss to combine over medium heat. Remove from the heat and add the cubes of cheese. Toss to combine, then scatter the basil leaves on top (tear if large) and serve immediately.

AFELTRA

PASTIFICIO GIUSEPPE AFELTRA IS LOCATED in Gragnano in the Campania region—the birthplace of dry pasta making. Afeltra has made dried semolina pasta in the same location since 1848. Afeltra also uses the classic techniques and tools of dried pasta. Pasta is made using bronze dies that give each piece a slightly roughened surface, and each shape is dried on a specific schedule timed to bring out the best in it. Drying is never rushed—it can take as long as two days for pasta to dry properly before it is packaged. Afeltra creates numerous different shapes, but some of its most popular are the classics: long thin spaghetti, squiggly fusilli, ruffled mafalde, and striped rigatoni. The pasta is made with semolina flour and locally sourced spring water. The company also makes olive oil, panettone, and DOP red wine.

PASTA CON ZUCCA E SCAMORZA
PASTA WITH SQUASH AND SCAMORZA

Serves 6 as a first course

Green zucchini and yellow summer squash make a lovely contrast in this summer dish, which is perfect for a relaxed al fresco dinner with friends. For a memorable evening, pair this first course with a well-chilled white wine, such as a Falanghina.

2 tablespoons extra virgin olive oil

4 cloves garlic, smashed

2 yellow summer squash, cut into ½-inch cubes

2 zucchini, cut into ½-inch cubes

Fine sea salt to taste

Freshly ground black pepper to taste

1 pint grape tomatoes, halved

Coarse sea salt for pasta cooking water

1 pound short dried semolina pasta, such as Vesuvio or penne

8 ounces scamorza cheese, cut into ½-inch cubes

¼ cup fresh mint leaves

1 cup grated Pecorino Romano

BRING a large pot of water to a boil for cooking the pasta.

PLACE the olive oil and the garlic cloves in a large sauté pan over medium heat. Cook the garlic in the olive oil, stirring frequently, until the garlic is soft (but do not allow it to brown). Remove and discard the garlic.

INCREASE the heat to medium-high and add the summer squash and zucchini cubes. Season lightly with salt and pepper. Cook them, stirring occasionally, until they have released any liquid and begin to brown slightly, about 6 minutes. Add the grape tomato halves and continue to cook until they, too, have released their liquid.

MEANWHILE, when the water in the large pot boils, add salt (see page 22), and then add the pasta. Cook, stirring frequently, until the pasta is al dente (see page 22). Drain the pasta and add it to the sauté pan to coat with the sauce. Toss vigorously over medium heat until combined, about 2 minutes.

REMOVE the pan from the heat and toss in the cubes of scamorza. Mix well, and then tear and sprinkle the mint leaves all around the pan. Sprinkle in the grated Pecorino, stir to incorporate, and serve immediately.

LA PASTA ATTORCIGLIATA

Twisting dried semolina pasta as it is extruded creates ridges and curves that result in pleasing mouth-feel, chewiness, and of course the all-important little nooks and crannies for capturing sauce ingredients.

FUSILLI GRANDI

Larger fusilli provide generous curved pathways for collecting sauce, especially chunky sauces.

CASARECCE

Casarecce are gently twisted along two axes, both vertically (roughly into an S-shape) and horizontally. They are used throughout southern Italy and are particularly good with seafood dishes.

RADIATORI

A latecomer to the pasta world, radiatori (which resemble cast iron radiators) were developed between the two world wars. They are extremely effective at capturing sauces and toppings, as they are both cupped and deeply ridged.

FUSILLI

Fusilli, or "spindles," were once made at home by being wrapped around knitting needles. The corkscrew shape is one of our best sellers.

FARFALLE

Butterfly or bowtie pasta is pinched in the middle, which gives it a pleasant range of textures—the extreme ends are thin and silky, while the center "knot" is chewier. Farfalle pair well with oil-based sauces.

VESUVIO

Vesuvio pasta is named for the active volcano that looms over Napoli, but if you look carefully, they also resemble a shell to represent the seaside city.

FILEI

Like fusilli, Calabria's filei were once formed around knitting needles. They are like unsealed tubes, which allows the sauce to permeate the center very effectively. Filei are often served in spicy tomato sauce.

FUSILLI CON SPECK E RADICCHIO
FUSILLI WITH SPECK AND RADICCHIO

Serves 4 as a first course

This is the perfect dish to throw together when unexpected guests knock at your door. It can be made with fresh egg pasta (see page 68) for a somewhat more substantial dish, and it would be fabulous with fresh garganelli, a quill-shaped egg pasta. You can also serve grated Grana Padano cheese (see page 87) on the side if you like. Any variety of radicchio will work here. When radicchio cooks, it loses much of its bitterness and turns slightly sweet, a flavor that plays off the smokiness of the speck very well. Tip: Purchase the speck for this dish in a single slab and then cut it into cubes at home.

1 small head radicchio

2 ounces speck

1 shallot

1 tablespoon extra virgin olive oil

Fine sea salt to taste

¾ cup heavy cream

Coarse sea salt for pasta cooking water

1 pound fusilli

Freshly ground black pepper to taste

BRING a large pot of water to a boil for the pasta.

CUT the radicchio into ribbons. Chop the speck into ¼-inch cubes. Mince the shallot.

IN a skillet large enough to hold the pasta comfortably, heat the olive oil over medium heat. Add the shallot and speck and cook, stirring frequently, until the shallot is translucent, about 3 minutes.

ADD the radicchio and stir to combine. Season lightly with fine sea salt. (Remember that the speck is somewhat salty.) Turn the heat to low and cook, covered, until the radicchio is very wilted and has turned dark purple, about 7 minutes. (If the radicchio starts to stick to the pan before it is cooked, add 1 to 2 tablespoons water.) Add the cream to the pan, stir, and cook until just slightly reduced and clinging to the radicchio, about 3 minutes.

MEANWHILE, when the water in the large pot boils, add coarse salt (see page 22) and then add the fusilli. Cook, stirring frequently with a wooden spoon, until the pasta is al dente. (See page 22 for more on the proper cooking technique for dried pasta.)

WHEN the pasta is al dente, drain in a colander and then transfer to the pan with the sauce. Toss over medium heat until the pasta is coated in sauce. Season with a generous amount of fresh pepper and serve immediately.

VESUVIO AL RAGÙ DI SALSICCIA E SCAROLA

VESUVIO PASTA WITH SAUSAGE RAGÙ AND ESCAROLE

Serves 6 as a first course

Vesuvio (named for the still-active volcano on whose slopes the city of Napoli was built) is a short curly pasta that resembles shells, representing the seaside city. Each piece has numerous nooks and crannies that make it a great match for a chunky sauce like this one, which is a Neapolitan-style ragù rather than the Bolognese-style ragù served over tagliatelle on page 94. Just be sure to use plain sausage for this pasta, not the type with fennel or hot pepper in it, which would overwhelm the other flavors. As with the Bolognese ragù, you want to cook the meat very gently rather than browning it.

12 ounces sweet sausage

1 tablespoon red wine

1 cup tomato puree

½ cup chicken or beef stock

3 cups shredded escarole

Fine sea salt to taste

Coarse sea salt for pasta cooking water

1 pound Vesuvio pasta or other short pasta, preferably with a complex shape

3 tablespoons extra virgin olive oil

Grated Grana Padano cheese (see page 87) for serving

REMOVE the sausage casings and crumble the meat into a small bowl. Sprinkle the wine over the meat and massage the wine into the meat by hand until it is soft and elastic, about 2 minutes.

PLACE the meat in a cold skillet with high sides. Place the skillet over low heat and slowly cook the meat until it is no longer raw looking, about 2 minutes. Do not brown the meat.

ADD the tomato puree and stir to combine. Increase the heat until the tomato puree is simmering gently.

POUR in the stock, stir once, and decrease the heat until the ragù is at a very gentle simmer, with a bubble just occasionally breaking the surface. Simmer, uncovered, without stirring for 2 hours. The meat should poach in the liquid and turn very soft.

WHEN the sauce is cooked, carefully spoon off and discard any liquid remaining on the top. Stir in the escarole and cook until just wilted, about 2 minutes. Season to taste with fine sea salt. Remove from the heat.

BRING a large pot of water to a boil. When the water is boiling, salt it with coarse sea salt (see page 22) and add the pasta. Cook the pasta until al dente (see page 22).

SMEAR a small amount of the sauce on the bottom of a warmed pasta serving bowl.

WHEN the pasta is cooked, drain it in a colander, then transfer it immediately to the serving bowl. Top with the remaining sauce and toss vigorously to combine. Drizzle on the olive oil and toss again. Serve immediately with grated cheese on the side.

MAFALDINE CON FUNGHI, TIMO E MASCARPONE

MAFALDINE WITH MUSHROOMS, THYME, AND MASCARPONE

Serves 4 as a first course

Mafaldine are wide ribbons with ruffled edges. They're one of the prettiest pasta shapes and are often paired with vegetable sauces. Use a combination of mushrooms for the maximum amount of flavor: oyster, shiitake, and maitake are all good options.

¼ cup extra virgin olive oil

1 pound mushrooms, sliced

1 shallot, finely diced

Fine sea salt and freshly ground black pepper

2 tablespoons minced fresh thyme leaves

1 pinch crushed red pepper flakes

Coarse sea salt for pasta cooking water

1 pound mafaldine

¼ cup mascarpone

½ cup grated Grana Padano (see page 87) cheese

BRING a large pot of water to a boil. Meanwhile, heat a large skillet with high sides over high heat and add the olive oil. Once the oil is hot, add the mushrooms and cook, stirring frequently, until they are lightly golden, about 8 minutes. Add the shallot, season with salt and pepper and mix well to combine. Add the thyme and red pepper flakes, then turn down the heat to low.

WHEN the water is boiling, season with coarse salt, add the pasta and cook al dente. (See page 22.) Remove the pasta from the water, reserving cooking water, and add it to the skillet. Turn the heat up to medium-high and cook the pasta, tossing constantly, until combined, about 2 minutes. Add pasta cooking water in small amounts if necessary.

REMOVE the skillet from the heat and stir in the mascarpone and grated cheese. Toss and adjust seasoning. Toss again, incorporating a small amount of pasta cooking water if the pasta looks dry. Serve immediately.

➤ Never soak fresh mushrooms. Simply brush with a damp paper towel and shake them over the sink to remove any grit.

CROXETTI AL PESTO GENOVESE
CROXETTI PASTA WITH PESTO

Serves 6 as a first course

The cuisine of Liguria is famed for its herb-heavy dishes, chief among them pesto. A proper pesto hits your nose with the scent of basil, which can only be described as intensely green. A pesto is literally a paste and is never cooked. Pesto Genovese is the best-known example (see page 54). Croxetti are coin-shaped disks of pasta produced with special stamps that imprint the disks with symbols. You can use another type of dried pasta in this recipe, or pair with fresh egg pasta.

Coarse sea salt for cooking water

8 ounces green beans

2 small Yukon gold potatoes, peeled and sliced about ¾ inch thick

1 pound croxetti pasta (see page 55)

1 clove garlic

Fine sea salt to taste

Leaves of 1 bunch fresh basil (about 2 loosely packed cups)

2 tablespoons pine nuts

½ cup extra virgin olive oil

½ cup grated Pecorino Romano

BRING a large pot of water to a boil.

WHEN the water is boiling, add coarse salt. Add the green beans and cook until tender, about 5 minutes. Remove with a slotted spoon. Add the potato slices and cook until tender enough to be pierced easily with a paring knife but not falling apart, about 8 minutes. Remove with a slotted spoon to a warmed large serving bowl.

ADD the pasta to the pot, and cook, stirring frequently with a wooden spoon, until the croxetti are cooked. (See page 22 for more on the proper cooking technique for dried pasta.)

WHILE the pasta is cooking, cut the green beans into 1-inch pieces and add to the serving bowl with the potatoes.

PLACE the garlic and a generous pinch of fine sea salt in a large mortar and grind against the sides until crushed into a paste. Add about a quarter of the basil leaves and grind until broken down. Continue to add the basil a little at a time, breaking down all the leaves before adding more. Add the pine nuts and grind until crushed. Add the olive oil and grind until the pesto is creamy. Finally, add the cheese and smooth until creamy and thoroughly combined.

STIR about 2 tablespoons of the pasta cooking water into the pesto. Add a little of the pesto to the serving bowl and toss with the potatoes and green beans.

WHEN the pasta is cooked, drain it and add it to the serving bowl. Top with the remaining pesto, toss to combine thoroughly, and serve hot.

SALSA CLASSICA: PESTO GENOVESE

OH, PESTO, what sins have been committed in thy name! We've seen it slathered everywhere, and in all kinds of bastardized forms. *Pesto* simply means paste but pesto Genovese is made with basil and pine nuts as described below.

Basil—especially the small-leafed Genovese basil that grows along the coast of Liguria—smells green and summery. Pesto is never cooked, but when it is served over pasta a little of the pasta cooking water can be incorporated into it at the last minute. Pesto is always best prepared just before you plan to use it. It is also best ground by hand in a mortar and pestle. It's not difficult, we promise!

Makes about 1 cup pesto

1 clove garlic
Fine sea salt to taste
Leaves of 1 bunch fresh basil (about 2 loosely packed cups)
2 tablespoons pine nuts
½ cup extra virgin olive oil
½ cup grated Pecorino Romano

Place the garlic and a generous pinch of salt in a large mortar and grind against the sides until crushed into a paste. Add about a quarter of the basil leaves and grind until broken down. Continue to add the basil a little at a time, breaking down all the leaves before adding more. Add the pine nuts and grind until crushed. Add the oil and grind until the pesto is creamy. Finally, add the cheese and grind until creamy and thoroughly combined.

DUE FACCE DELLA STESSA MONETA

Croxetti, or corzetti, is the name for two different types of pasta that are two sides of the same coin—both are dried pastas that are "minted" by being pressed or stamped rather than rolled out. They are native to northern Liguria rather than Campania, home base for most of the dried pasta in Italy, and the techniques for making them may actually have arrived from France.

CROXETTI DELLA VAL POLCEVERA

These smaller croxetti are made in the shape of the numeral eight or an infinity symbol. Despite their small size, they are never eaten in soup, only in sauces. Though originally they were made by hand to resemble twisted orecchiette (and you can still find handmade versions in the valley of the Polcevera river), these days they are more likely to be punched out of a thin sheet of dough like their larger siblings.

CROXETTI DEL LEVANTE

These disks resemble coins, and are often stamped with a design on either side. (Corzetti were Genovese currency used in the fourteenth century.) Corzetti were once imprinted with the coats of arms of various families and you still will find them with various symbols embossed on them in relief. These days they're more likely to have the pasta maker's logo! This tradition dates back to the Middle Ages, and beautiful wooden stamps for making them can still be found in Liguria. Their surface is fairly coarse-grained.

LE PASTINE

Small pasta is most often cooked in either brothy or chunky soups, though there are a few *pasta asciutta* (pasta with sauce) dishes that call for small-size pieces. Many of the small pasta varieties are just smaller versions of larger pasta shapes. The suffix *-ino* (plural *-ini*) at the end of an Italian word means "small."

Pasta in soup is almost always cooked directly in the broth. Bring the liquid to a boil and stir in the pasta just as you would if cooking it in water. The soup should be a little thinner than you would like (add water if needed) to start as it will thicken as the pasta cooks, both because the liquid will reduce and because starch will be released from the pasta.

BRICHETTI

Brichetti is dialect for "matchsticks" in Genova, where this pasta originated. Brichetti are most often served in Liguria's famed minestrone. (See page 59.)

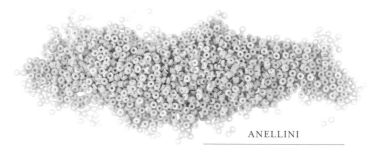

ANELLINI

Like all diminutive pasta, these "little rings" from Sicilia are delicious in soup, but in Palermo they appear in a classic baked pasta dish with a sauce of tomato, peas, and meat (see page 58). These are sometimes labeled anelletti.

DITALINI

*A ditale is a thimble used to protect a thumb
while sewing. Ditalini pasta are like penne
or other tubular pasta cut into short lengths.
They may be either lisci, "smooth," or rigati,
"ridged," and are great with all types of soup.*

RISONI

*Risoni resemble grains of rice. They are occasionally
labeled orzo, or barley. They are sometimes used in
place of rice in a traditional vegetable rice salad and
are a good choice for cooking pasta risotto style.*

FARFALLINE

*Just ½ inch or so long, tiny butterflies are best for
soup. They look especially charming floating in a
bowl of broth and are always a favorite with kids.*

ANELLETTI PALERMITANI
AL FORNO
BAKED RING PASTA WITH RAGÙ AND PEAS

Serves 6 to 8 as a first course

This dish is sometimes prepared as a timballo (in a springform pan lined with parchment), or baked under a "lid" of thinly rolled pizza dough.

2 tablespoons extra virgin olive oil, plus more for oiling pan

½ cup breadcrumbs (see page 87)

1 large red Tropea onion, minced

8 ounces ground beef

8 ounces ground pork

½ cup red wine

2 cups tomato puree

2 cups shelled peas

Fine sea salt and freshly ground black pepper to taste

Coarse sea salt for cooking pasta

1 pound anelletti pasta

1 cup grated caciocavallo cheese

¾ cup diced primosale cheese

PREHEAT the oven to 350°F. Oil a 9-by-13-inch baking dish and coat the bottom and sides with about half of the breadcrumbs. Set aside.

IN a large pot, sauté the onion in the 2 tablespoons olive oil until golden. Add the ground beef and pork and break up with a fork. Cook until the meat begins to brown, then add the wine and cook until it has evaporated. Add the tomato puree and the peas, season with salt and pepper, and simmer until tomato has reduced and peas are soft, about 20 minutes.

MEANWHILE, bring a large pot of water to a boil. Season with coarse salt. Add the pasta and cook until fairly al dente. (See page 22.) Drain the pasta and add to the pot with the sauce. Stir to combine. Stir in ¾ cup of the grated caciocavallo and all of the primosale. Taste and adjust seasoning.

TRANSFER the pasta mixture to the prepared pan and smooth the top with a spatula. Sprinkle on the remaining grated cheese and the remaining breadcrumbs and bake until golden brown on top and cooked through, about 30 minutes. Let the pasta settle for 5 to 10 minutes before serving.

➤ You can use either fresh shelled peas or frozen peas for the sauce. If using frozen peas, there's no need to defrost them.

MINESTRONE ALLA GENOVESE
GENOVA MINESTRONE

Serves 4 as a first course

A minestra is a soup, and a minestrone is a big and hearty soup. Almost every region in Italy has its own version. This Ligurian version incorporates a dollop of pesto.

1 clove garlic

1 potato, peeled and diced

2 zucchini, diced

2 cups shredded Savoy cabbage

½ cup shelled peas

2 carrots, diced

1 cup green beans, cut into 1-inch lengths

1 cup dried borlotti beans, soaked for 8 hours and drained, or fresh shelled borlotti beans

Fine sea salt and freshly ground black pepper to taste

12 ounces (about 2 cups) bricchetti or ditalini or other small pasta

¼ cup pesto alla Genovese (see page 54)

2 tablespoons extra virgin olive oil

Grated Grana Padano cheese (see page 87) for serving

COMBINE the garlic, potato, zucchini, cabbage, peas, carrots, green beans, and borlotti in a soup pot and add enough water to cover the vegetables by 2 inches. Bring to a boil, then turn down to a simmer and simmer until beans and vegetables are soft, about 1 hour. Season with salt and pepper.

IF the soup is overly thick, thin with a little water. Stir in the pasta and simmer until pasta is cooked through. To serve, place 1 tablespoon of pesto in the bottom of each of 4 individual serving plates. Ladle the soup on top, then drizzle the oil on top. Serve with grated cheese on the side.

➤ The variations are endless. Stick to seasonal vegetables and you will always end up with a tasty minestrone. You can also puree some or all of the cooked vegetables and beans if you like.

LE PERLE DEL MEDITERRANEO

Not all dried semolina pasta is extruded. Couscous and fregola are both semolina pasta made by rubbing hard wheat flour with water until small balls form. You can make your own rubbed semolina pasta at home, or you can purchase high-quality versions at Eataly. The cooking process for these types of pasta is different than that for traditional dried semolina pasta.

FREGOLA GRANDE

Standard fregola is irregular in size and shape, but rarely larger than $1/10$ inch in diameter. Fregola grande is about twice as big. Though fregola of all sizes is similar to couscous, no one is certain whether the two share common origins. Fregola may be a truly indigenous food, or it may have been introduced to Sardegna by the Phoenicians or the Carthaginians many centuries ago.

FREGOLA

Fregola comes from Italy's second largest island, Sardegna. The name derives from the Latin ferculum, *meaning to break something down into small pieces. Fregola is similar to couscous but has a rougher surface, and the semolina flour for fregola is toasted, which gives it a nutty accent. Like malloreddus (see page 116), fregola may include a pinch or two of saffron for flavor. Fregola is most often paired with shellfish, especially clams.*

COUSCOUS

Couscous is usually smooth and comes in a variety of sizes, but the tiny couscous that resembles cracked wheat is the type most commonly found on Sicilia. It is eaten on the western side of Sicilia, which has a heavy Arab influence. Couscous is both the name of the pasta and the name of the finished dish, which is almost always prepared with shellfish.

INSALATA DI FREGOLA
CON CALAMARI E CECI

FREGOLA SALAD WITH CALAMARI AND CHICKPEAS

Serves 4 as a main course

Fregola is Sardegna's answer to couscous—a toasted semolina-flour pasta formed into little balls. Its rough surface is perfect for soaking up liquid, and it is served in room-temperature salads and in soups. Sardegna, of course, is an island, so it's natural that its signature pasta is frequently paired with seafood, particularly clams, mussels, and calamari. Fregola is sometimes made with a little saffron.

1½ pounds calamari

Coarse sea salt for cooking water

8 ounces fregola

¼ cup extra virgin olive oil

1 cup cooked chickpeas

1 small red onion, minced

Juice of ½ lemon

1 clove garlic, minced

2 tablespoons minced fresh flat-leaf parsley

2 tablespoons minced fresh oregano leaves

Fine sea salt to taste

Freshly ground black pepper to taste

CUT the calamari tentacles in half the long way and slice the bodies into rings.

BRING a large pot of water to a boil. Salt the water with coarse sea salt (see page 22), add the calamari, and cook just until opaque, about 30 seconds. Remove with a slotted spoon or skimmer.

ADD the fregola to the water and cook as for pasta, stirring frequently, until the fregola is al dente, about 10 minutes. Drain, toss with 1 tablespoon olive oil, and set aside to cool.

COMBINE the calamari, chickpeas, red onion, and cooked fregola in a large bowl. In a small bowl, whisk together the remaining 3 tablespoons olive oil, the lemon juice, garlic, parsley, and oregano. Season with a little fine sea salt and pepper and pour the vinaigrette over the salad. Toss to combine.

SERVE at room temperature.

COUSCOUS ALLA TRAPANESE
SEAFOOD COUSCOUS FROM TRAPANI

Serves 6 to 8 as a first course

Trapani was under Arab domain for 270 years beginning in 827, and its culture and cuisine still reflect that influence. Any fish that doesn't make its way into this dish would likely appear as part of the second course that follows in a traditional Italian meal.

1 large whole white fish, such as scorpionfish, filleted with bones reserved

6 large shrimp, peeled and deveined, peels reserved

1 rib celery

1 carrot

1 bay leaf

2 yellow onions

1 pound small clams

1 pound mussels

½ cup white wine

¼ cup extra virgin olive oil

1 clove garlic, minced

¼ teaspoon crushed red pepper flakes

1 cup peeled tomatoes, crushed by hand

Fine sea salt and freshly ground black pepper to taste

1 pinch saffron threads

¼ cup ground blanched almonds

8 ounces couscous

¼ cup chopped fresh flat-leaf parsley

CUT fish fillets into large strips and set aside. In a pot combine the shrimp shells, fish bones and head, celery, carrot, bay leaf, and one of the onions. Add 4 cups water and simmer for 45 minutes. Strain and set aside. You should have at least 1 cup broth.

PLACE the clams and mussels in a large skillet over high heat. Add the wine and cover. Cook until shellfish have opened, 4 to 5 minutes. Remove shellfish from shells and set aside. Strain the cooking liquid that remains in the skillet and add it to the broth.

MINCE the remaining onion. In a medium pot, sauté the onion in the olive oil until golden, then add the garlic and red pepper flakes. Sauté until fragrant, then add the tomatoes. Bring to a brisk simmer and add the pieces of fish fillet. Season with salt and pepper and add the saffron and almonds. When the fish flakes easily, stir in the shrimp and cook until they are opaque, 2 to 3 minutes.

PLACE the couscous in a heatproof bowl. Bring the reserved broth to a boil, then pour 1 cup of hot broth over the couscous. Stir with a fork to combine. Cover the bowl and let the couscous rest for 5 minutes. Fluff with a fork. If the couscous is not tender, continue to add hot broth in small amounts, letting it sit between additions, until it is ready.

TO serve, divide the couscous between individual serving dishes. Top each portion with some of the fish and tomato mixture and the reserved clams and mussels. Sprinkle on parsley. Pass any remaining broth on the side.

SPAGHETTI DI FARRO CON CARCIOFI

FARRO PENNE WITH ARTICHOKES

Serves 4 as a first course

Rich farro pasta makes even a simple and light vegetable dish feel filling and satisfying.

¼ cup extra virgin olive oil

1 yellow onion, diced

6 to 8 baby artichokes

Fine sea salt and freshly ground black pepper to taste

Coarse sea salt for pasta cooking water

1 pound farro penne

6 leaves fresh basil, torn

Grated Grana Padano cheese (see page 87) for serving

BRING a large pot of water to a boil for cooking the pasta.

MEANWHILE, in a skillet, heat the olive oil over medium-low heat and gently sauté the onion until golden. Add the artichoke, turn up the heat to medium-high, and cook, stirring frequently, until browned. Season with salt and pepper and remove from the heat.

WHEN the water is boiling, season with coarse sea salt and cook the pasta al dente. (See page 22.) Drain the pasta and add to the skillet with the artichoke. Toss over high heat until combined, about 2 minutes, adding a little pasta cooking water if necessary to keep the skillet from drying out. Remove from heat and scatter the basil on top. Serve immediately with grated cheese on the side.

HOW TO TRIM AN ARTICHOKE

1. Fill a large bowl with water and the juice of 1 lemon.

2. Remove any leaves from the artichoke stem, and then cut the stem, leaving an inch or two. Pull off and discard any hard, dark-colored leaves.

3. When you have revealed the light green portion of the artichoke, peel any tough skin off the outside of the stem.

4. Cut off the top of the artichoke's leaves.

5. If leaving the artichoke whole, place it upside down on the counter and press down firmly to open it up. Use a small paring knife to cut out and discard the hairy choke. If slicing the artichoke, cut it in half the long way, then into quarters, and simply cut out the choke with a paring knife (as if coring an apple or pear).

6. Drop the artichoke into the lemon water and repeat with the remaining artichokes.

CEREALI ANTICHI

Ancient grains or heirloom grains are strains that fell out of favor over time, often because they were not as easy to farm in large amounts. In recent years they've been rediscovered, though it's a little funny to think of something that's been around for centuries—in some cases millennia—as "trendy." Ancient grains are usually milled into whole grain flours rather than refined flours; the pasta made with them tends to have an assertive flavor of its own, which makes it stand out more than standard pasta made with refined semolina flour.

TAJARIN DI CASTAGNE

Gluten-free chestnut flour is made by grinding dried chestnuts. It has long been used in Italy to make not only pasta, but also cakes and porridges. Chestnuts are not actually a grain, but chestnut flour pasta, such as chestnut tajarin, shares many of the characteristics of pasta made with ancient grains.

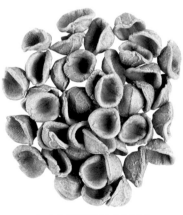

ORECCHIETTE D'ARSO

Arso means "burnt" and that's literally what it is—the charred remains of wheat left in the field after farmers torched it to prepare to plant the following year's harvest, similar to the process that first gave rise to freekeh in the Middle East. In Puglia, chefs began incorporating this nutty-tasting grain into pasta, especially the region's famed orecchiette. The complex, slightly bitter flavor goes particularly well with shellfish.

PENNE DI FARRO

This short farro penne pairs especially well with mushrooms and artichokes.

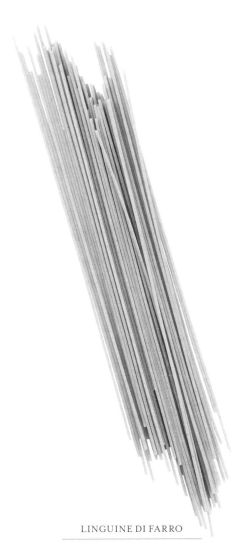

GRAMIGNA DI KAMUT

Kamut is an ancient wheat that developed in what is now Iran. It is generally more nutritious than modern wheat. It has a naturally buttery flavor that pairs well with butter-based sauces.

LINGUINE DI FARRO

The Etruscans, our early Italian ancestors, ate farro wheat. Farro can be used to make all kinds of pasta, from fresh to dried. Farro linguine works well with shellfish dishes.

PASTA
FRESCA

Making your own pasta elevates any dish.

How to Make Egg Pasta

EGG PASTA IS THE MOST COMMON FORM OF FRESH PASTA IN ITALY and is eaten throughout central and northern Italy. Egg pasta is not difficult to make, and it uses only two ingredients, which you likely already have on hand: unbleached all-purpose flour and eggs.

You will need 1 large egg and about 1 cup flour per portion. Start with ¾ cup flour for each egg and then add as you go along. You will need a large wooden work surface (in Italy, most home kitchens are equipped with a board that has a lip that hangs over the side of the counter to hold it in place), a bench scraper, and a straight dowel rolling pin if you are rolling out the dough by hand (preferable, but it takes practice) or a crank pasta machine. Egg pasta is also used to make stuffed pasta and *pasta al forno*, or baked pasta.

1. Form the flour into a well on the work surface or in a bowl. (In a bowl is easier and recommended the first few times you try this.) Crack the eggs into the well, and with the index and middle finger of one hand or with a small fork, whisk the eggs. Gradually draw in flour from the sides of the well until the egg has been absorbed by the flour. With a bench scraper, set the dough off to the side.

2. Clean off your hands, adding any dough scraps to the dough, and wash your hands. Clean the work surface, first by scraping it with the bench scraper, and then by wiping it with a damp cloth or sponge. (If you began by kneading the dough in a bowl, you don't need to perform this step.) Lightly flour the work surface.

3. Transfer the dough to the lightly floured part of the work surface. Knead the dough. The weather, the age of your flour, the size of your eggs, and numerous other factors can influence the dough's texture. If the dough is dry and crumbly, sprinkle it with lukewarm water until it becomes pliable. If it is so wet that it is unwieldy, add flour, about a tablespoon at a time, until you can handle it. Continue kneading the dough until smooth, about 10 minutes. When you cut through the dough with a knife, you should see a consistent color and texture, not whorls of flour and/or egg.

4. Clean off the work surface with a bench scraper. Set the dough to the side on the work surface, cover with an overturned bowl (if you used a bowl above, just rinse it out and use it here), and allow to rest for 30 minutes. This is probably the most important step in making egg pasta dough—don't try to skip it.

5. Cut off a piece of pasta dough the size of an egg. Leave the remaining dough covered under the overturned bowl.

(continued)

When you cut into the dough, it's good to see layers, but you do not want to see bits of flour or egg.

To roll by hand, start at the center of the dough and roll toward the outer edges.

6. *To roll pasta dough by hand:* Shape the dough into a rough circle. Lightly flour the clean work surface. Begin rolling the dough as you would a pastry crust, starting in the center and rolling away from you to the outer edge. Turn the ball of dough a quarter-turn and repeat all the way around, then continue rolling, turning the dough about one-eighth of the way around, until the sheet of dough is ⅛ inch thin or less. Scatter a small amount of flour on the dough any time it threatens to stick to the surface or the rolling pin. Finish thinning the sheet of dough by wrapping three-quarters of the sheet around the rolling pin toward you, then rapidly unrolling it while running your hands across the sheet of dough, from the center of the rolling pin to the ends. Press out and away from you with the rolling pin. Continue to do this, turning the dough between rolls, until the sheet is extremely thin (see Note).

   To roll pasta dough using a crank machine: Pass the piece of dough between the smooth rollers on the widest setting. Fold the piece of dough in half and pass it through again, fold it, and pass it through a third time. It should be smooth. Proceed to thin the pasta dough through the smooth rollers by decreasing the setting between rolls. In other words, if 10 is the widest setting on your machine, now decrease the setting to 9 and pass the piece of dough through. This time, do not fold it, but decrease the setting step-by-step until you have thinned the dough to the desired thickness, usually the thinnest setting, but see below for some exceptions. Set the thinned pasta dough aside for about 10 minutes while you repeat with the remaining dough. Arrange the sheet of dough on a table or counter so that about one-third is hanging over the edge while you repeat with the remaining dough.

7. *To cut hand-rolled pasta dough into shapes:* Clean and very lightly flour the work surface. Spread out a clean flat-weave dish towel on the counter and set aside. Gently roll the first sheet of dough around the rolling pin and slip it off the rolling pin and onto the work surface. (It should be a flat roll.) Cut the roll of dough into strips the desired width, then gently lift them in the air and let them drop onto the dish towel to separate them. Repeat with remaining sheets of dough. (Flour the cut strips lightly if they threaten to stick, though by now they should be fairly dry.)

   To cut machine-rolled pasta dough into shapes: The surface of the sheets of dough should feel very dry and matte. Flour them lightly and pass the dough through the notched rollers for strips, or cut it by hand into the desired shape.

   NOTE: Tradition dictates that the sheet of dough should be transparent enough that if you lay it over a newspaper, you can read the newsprint through it. Since that's not a very sanitary practice, to determine whether or not the sheet of dough is thin enough, slide your hand underneath and check whether you can see it.

To use a hand-cranked machine, pass the dough through several times to ensure smoothness.

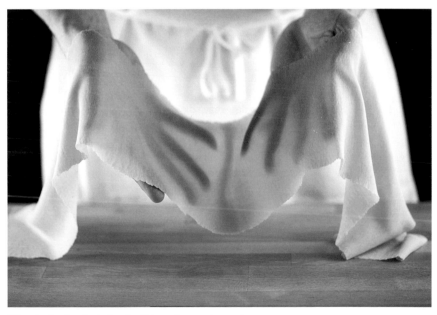

When the dough is finished, it should be so thin as to be translucent.

PASSATELLI IN BRODO

BREADCRUMB PASTA IN BROTH

Serves 6 as a first course

In Italy, you can purchase a special type of food mill for creating breadcrumb pasta, or *passatelli,* but a potato ricer with large holes works fine. If you like thicker strands, you can also roll them out by hand. (First shape them into ropes about ¼ inch thick, then cut them into strands.) The hand-rolled pasta will cook in about 5 minutes. This is traditionally served in capon broth or beef broth, but it's delicious in chicken broth, too.

1½ quarts beef or poultry broth (see page 74)

⅔ cup grated Grana Padano or Parmigiano Reggiano, plus more for serving

1½ cups fine plain (unflavored) breadcrumbs (see page 87), plus more as needed

Grated zest of 1 lemon

½ teaspoon freshly grated nutmeg

2 large eggs, lightly beaten

BRING the broth to a boil in a large pot.

IN a bowl, combine the cheese, breadcrumbs, lemon zest, and nutmeg. Make a well in the center of the mixture and add the eggs. Mix by hand until thoroughly combined. The dough should be damp but firm. You may need to incorporate additional breadcrumbs or a few drops of water.

PLACE about half the dough in a potato ricer fitted with the attachment with the largest holes. Squeeze the dough so that the shapes are extruded. Cut them off in 3-inch lengths, letting them drop directly into the boiling broth. Repeat with the remaining dough.

GENTLY stir the passatelli and cook until they float to the surface, about 2 minutes. Ladle broth and pasta into individual serving bowls. Serve additional grated cheese on the side.

BROTH BUDDIES

PASTA AND BROTH—IT'S A MATCH MADE IN HEAVEN. Many different forms of pasta can be served in broth, but there is a common theme: small size. Tiny egg pasta—*quadretti* (little squares), confetti, and the like—are always a solid choice for thickening a soup. When you make any type of egg pasta, chop the scraps into little squares or irregularly shaped small pieces, then transfer those to a sealable bag and store for several months in the freezer. You can cook them directly in broth without defrosting them first. The next time you are trying to transform a bowl of soup into a full meal, you'll be glad to have small pasta at the ready.

There are also other kinds of egg pasta specifically made for broth, such as garganelli (see page 92) and passatelli (opposite). Tortellini in broth is one of the signature dishes of Bologna.

HOW TO MAKE BROTH

FIRST OF ALL, although people tend to use the words interchangeably, there is a difference between broth and stock. Broth is made with meat; stock is made with bones. Stock is most frequently used as an ingredient in other dishes. When you want a bowl of soup to slurp, you want broth.

Because broth is made using meat, when you have finished making it you will have the cook's treat: *lesso,* or boiled meat. That sounds prosaic, but boiled beef and chicken are delicious and useful. You can debone and skin the meat and then shred it back into the resulting broth for a heartier soup, or you can serve it as a second course (as in the *bollito misto* much beloved in Piemonte). It's delicious sprinkled with salt and drizzled with good olive oil, or you can serve an herb sauce alongside for added zing.

Making broth couldn't be easier. All it requires is time and a relatively large pot. Broth freezes so beautifully that it makes sense to prepare a big batch, and a good stockpot is an investment you will never regret.

You can make beef broth, chicken broth, or a broth that combines poultry and beef, which is fairly common in Italy. Place the meat in a large stockpot with water to cover by several inches. Bring to a boil over high heat, then reduce the heat to achieve a gentle simmer. Skim off any foam that clumps on the top, and continue to skim any foam that appears (after the first 30 minutes or so you won't see any more). As flavorings, add any or all of the following to the pot: a few chopped carrots, a few chopped stalks of celery, a crushed garlic clove or two, one or two peeled and chopped onions, parsley sprigs, bay leaves. Salt very lightly. The broth will reduce as it cooks and the saltiness will grow more concentrated. Cover the pot with the lid askew and simmer gently until the meat is fork tender and falling off the bone, at least 1½ hours, but preferably longer. It is impossible to overcook broth.

Fat is a necessary component of broth. Do not even dream of making broth with skinless chicken or lean cuts of meat. For chicken broth, use a whole chicken. You don't need to bother to cut it up. For beef broth, we like a combination of shank and shoulder. Whether using poultry or beef, it is very important that it be on the bone—the bones contribute collagen. You can also make a vegetarian broth using just the flavorings listed above and omitting the meat. It will never have the same rich flavor, but it can be a light and refreshing change from beef broth. Simply cook the vegetables until they are quite soft and have given up their flavor, about 45 minutes.

At this point, strain the broth through a fine sieve. If it still looks cloudy, you may want to strain it a second time. Take any meat off the bone and reserve it for another use. If the broth seems excessively greasy, refrigerate it—the fat will form a solid raft on top of the liquid, and you can easily remove it. Do not remove all of the fat, however. A few *occhi,* or eyes, of fat floating on the surface are the sign of a good broth. Broth will keep in the refrigerator in a tightly closed container for several days. It also freezes extremely well.

GRATTINI ALL'UOVO IN BRODO
GRATED EGG DUMPLINGS IN BROTH

Serves 6

These dumplings are tiny. Indeed, they are so small that they will cook almost instantly when added to hot broth. Some cooks like to ladle the hot broth over uncooked dumplings in serving bowls and let them cook that way, but we find the stovetop method slightly more reliable. Serve with a little extra grated cheese on the side if you like.

2 cups 00 flour or unbleached all-purpose flour

1 large egg

1 egg yolk

¼ cup grated Parmigiano Reggiano or Grana Padano cheese

Fine sea salt to taste

1½ quarts broth (see opposite)

WORK the flour, egg, egg yolk, grated cheese, and a little salt into a well-combined dough, following steps 1 through 4 on page 68.

AFTER the dough has rested, place a four-sided grater on a clean kitchen towel and grate the dough on the largest holes to make small dumplings, letting them collect on the towel. Shake the towel to distribute the dumplings evenly in a single layer and allow them to dry for 1 to 2 hours.

WHEN you are ready to serve the soup, place the broth in a pot and bring to a boil. Add the dumplings, stir to combine, and wait for the dumplings to rise to the surface. They will probably do so as the broth returns to a boil. Turn off the heat and let the dumplings sit in the pot for 2 to 3 minutes. Adjust seasoning and serve.

Gnocchi di Tutti i Tipi

A *gnocco* (the singular of *gnocchi*) is a lump. If you bump your head in Italy, you may wake up the next morning with a *gnocco* marking the spot. *Gnocco* is also slang for a good-looking guy, though beware of using it—in some places it means someone who's a real idiot. There's an old Italian saying—*Ridi, ridi, che la mamma ha fatto i gnocchi*—that literally means, "Go ahead and laugh, your mother made gnocchi." That may sound nice (who doesn't want homemade gnocchi?), but it means you're so thick-headed you don't even know what you're laughing about.

In culinary terms, though, *gnocchi* are dumplings. The most common gnocchi are potato gnocchi, but they can also be made with cheese and with all kinds of vegetables—spinach and winter squash are both popular options. Whatever ingredients they incorporate, these little pillows of goodness are a treat and pair with a wide variety of sauces. Gnocchi are one of the easiest types of homemade pasta to create, as they do not require rolling out with a pin or a machine. You simply shape the dough into ropes and then cut the ropes into pieces. Don't skip rolling each piece against a ridged wooden board (see page 100) or the tines of a fork, however; creating these indented lines on the sides of the gnocchi is key to helping them capture the sauce. Small gnocchi may also be served in broth, and many recipes call for baking cooked gnocchi briefly, often with a scattering of grated cheese on top—a crisp browned crust always contrasts beautifully with tender gnocchi.

Potato gnocchi can be frozen. Pop them into the freezer on a baking sheet, then transfer them to a plastic freezer bag once they're hard. (If you put them in the bag to start they may stick together.) Don't defrost frozen gnocchi—just drop them directly into boiling water. Potato gnocchi don't keep well at room temperature, however, as they begin to exude liquid, so either freeze them or make them just before you plan to use them.

One of the great joys of gnocchi is that they are both light (when properly made) and filling. For years, Italians were encouraged to eat gnocchi on Thursdays, presumably because they would keep our bellies full on Friday, when Catholics were not supposed to eat meat. Many Roman osterie still serve gnocchi every Thursday in a nod to this tradition.

Giovedì gnocchi, venerdì pesce, sabato trippa.
Thursdays gnocchi, Fridays fish, Saturdays tripe.

Roll pieces of dough into ropes about ¾ inch in width.

Use a bench scraper or a sharp knife to cut the rope into little lumps, each about 1 inch in length.

GNOCCHI AL POMODORO PICCANTE

POTATO GNOCCHI WITH SPICY TOMATO SAUCE

Serves 6 as a first course

Pillowy potato gnocchi are the perfect mildly flavored canvas for a tomato sauce with a hit of *peperoncino*. They are also delicious matched with sharply flavored piccante Gorgonzola cheese. We like to roast the potatoes for our gnocchi rather than boiling them, as it keeps them from getting soggy. Gnocchi are some of the easiest fresh pasta to make. The only tricky part is not going overboard with the flour—add it gradually, as you may not need all 3 cups.

4 russet potatoes (about 1½ pounds total)

2 cups coarse sea salt, plus more for salting the pasta cooking water

3 cups unbleached all-purpose flour, plus more for dusting

1 tablespoon fine sea salt, plus more for seasoning the sauce

¼ cup extra virgin olive oil, plus more for finishing

2 cloves garlic, crushed

Pinch crushed red pepper flakes

1 (16-ounce) can whole peeled tomatoes

PREHEAT the oven to 350°F. Line a baking sheet with parchment paper and set aside.

SPRINKLE about ½ cup of the coarse salt in the bottom of a baking dish just large enough to hold the potatoes. Place the potatoes on the salt, then cover them with the remaining coarse salt. Bake in the preheated oven until easily pierced with a paring knife, about 40 minutes. Set aside to cool. (Discard the salt.)

ONCE the potatoes are cool enough to handle, peel them and mash them with a potato ricer. (You can use a fork, just be sure to crush them fairly thoroughly and not leave any large chunks.) On a work surface, spread the potatoes into a square about 10 by 10 inches.

IN a bowl, combine 2 cups of the flour and the 1 tablespoon fine sea salt. Sprinkle the flour mixture evenly over the potatoes.

KNEAD the potato mixture (use a bench scraper to help you get started, if necessary) until the mixture is uniform and forms a soft, still slightly sticky dough. If the dough is too sticky, add the remaining 1 cup flour in small amounts, but the less flour you manage to add, the lighter your gnocchi will be.

(continued)

79

WITH a knife, cut the dough into equal-size pieces roughly the size of an egg. Working one at a time, roll the pieces into ropes about ¾ inch wide. Cut the ropes into 1-inch pieces.

PICK UP one piece of the dough, roll it over the back of a fork, and let it drop onto the prepared baking sheet. Repeat with the remaining pieces of dough. The resulting gnocchi should be slightly curved with grooves that will capture the sauce. Dust the gnocchi lightly with flour and set aside.

PLACE the olive oil, garlic, and red pepper flakes in a saucepan and cook over medium heat until the garlic is fragrant and just light brown. Add the tomato juices and the tomatoes to the pan, crushing them by hand as you do (see photo, page 35). Season to taste with salt. Simmer the sauce until slightly thickened, about 20 minutes.

BRING a large pot of water to a boil for the gnocchi. When the water is boiling, salt it (see page 22), then add the gnocchi. Cook the gnocchi until they rise to the top of the water, about 1 minute. As they are finished cooking, remove them to a colander with a slotted spoon.

SPREAD a small amount of the tomato sauce on the bottom of a serving dish. Add the drained gnocchi, then spoon the remaining sauce on top. Toss to combine.

DRIZZLE with a little olive oil and serve immediately.

GNOCCHI CON FICHI

GNOCCHI WITH FIGS

Serves 8 as a first course

If you are lucky enough to find good fresh figs, you can use those in place of the dried figs and skip the rehydrating step. Fig balsamic and fig vin cotto (grape must cooked to a syrup) are ingredients that make a big impact even in small amounts. Either one adds a wonderful dimension to this dish.

½ pound dried figs

4 cups coarse sea salt, plus more for pasta cooking water

8 russet potatoes (about 3 pounds total)

2 cups 00 flour or unbleached all-purpose flour, plus more for dusting

2 tablespoons fine sea salt

1 large egg

1 egg yolk

½ teaspoon freshly grated nutmeg

8 tablespoons (1 stick) butter

¼ cup grated Parmigiano Reggiano, plus more for serving

1 tablespoon aged fig balsamic vinegar or fig vin cotto

PREHEAT the oven to 350°F. Line a baking sheet with parchment paper and set aside. Place the figs in a heat-proof bowl and add boiling water to cover by several inches. Set aside to soften.

SPRINKLE about a quarter of the coarse salt in the bottom of a baking dish just large enough to hold the potatoes. Cut slits in the potatoes. Place the potatoes on the salt, then cover them with the remaining coarse salt. Bake in the preheated oven until easily pierced with a paring knife, about 45 minutes. Set aside to cool. (Discard salt.)

ONCE the potatoes are cool enough to handle, peel them and mash them with a potato ricer. On a work surface, spread the potatoes out and allow to cool. Remove the figs from the soaking water, trim off the stems, and dice the figs.

IN a bowl, combine 2 cups of the flour and the fine sea salt with the potatoes, egg, yolk, and nutmeg. Knead until smooth and well combined. (You can also do this in a stand mixer with the paddle attachment on low speed.)

ON a floured work surface, roll a piece of the dough into a rope 1 inch in diameter, then cut into 1-inch pieces. Place one piece of fig in the center of one dumpling and press the fig into the dough so it is embedded. Roll the dumpling against a fork or paddle and let it drop onto the prepared baking sheet. Repeat with remaining dough and fig pieces. (You will probably not use all the fig pieces; reserve them.) Dust the prepared gnocchi lightly with flour and set aside.

BRING a pot of water to a boil for the gnocchi. Meanwhile, melt the butter in a large sauté pan. When the water is boiling, salt it and add the gnocchi. Whisk a little of the gnocchi cooking water into the melted butter, then add any remaining pieces of fig. Cook the gnocchi until they rise to the top of the water, about 1 minute. As they are finished cooking, remove them with a slotted spoon and add to the pan with the sauce. Cook the gnocchi, tossing gently, over medium heat for 2 minutes. Sprinkle in the cheese and toss to combine, then transfer to a serving bowl, drizzle with fig vinegar or vin cotto, and serve immediately.

GNOCCHI AL PARMIGIANO REGGIANO

GNOCCHI WITH THREE TYPES OF PARMIGIANO REGGIANO

Serves 6 as a first course

Forgive us if we sound love-struck when we talk about Parmigiano Reggiano, but it really is worthy of our praise and more. Like all cheeses, Parmigiano Reggiano develops different flavors as it ages—a wedge of cheese that has been aged for fourteen months will taste more mild and sweet than a cheese that has been aged for thirty-six months. This dish highlights those nuances by incorporating Parmigiano Reggiano of three different ages—an intergenerational party that really showcases this cheese that comes from the area around Parma.

GNOCCHI

2 to 3 russet potatoes (about 1 pound)

1½ cups coarse sea salt

1 large egg, lightly beaten

¼ cup 00 flour or unbleached all-purpose flour

1½ teaspoons fine sea salt

FONDUTA

½ cup heavy cream

1 cup grated 14-month Parmigiano Reggiano

FINISHING

4 tablespoons (½ stick) unsalted butter

Coarse sea salt for pasta cooking water

¼ cup grated 18-month Parmigiano Reggiano

4 ounces 36-month Parmigiano Reggiano, crumbled

PREHEAT the oven to 350°F. Line a baking sheet with parchment paper and set aside.

SPRINKLE about one-fourth of the coarse salt in the bottom of a baking dish just large enough to hold the potatoes. Place the potatoes on the salt, then cover them with the remaining coarse salt. Bake in the preheated oven until easily pierced with a paring knife, about 40 minutes. Set aside to cool. (Discard salt.)

ONCE the potatoes are cool enough to handle, peel them and mash them with a potato ricer. (You can use a fork, just be sure to crush them fairly thoroughly and not leave any large chunks.) Combine the potatoes, egg, flour, and fine sea salt. Knead until well combined, but do not overwork.

WITH a knife cut the dough into equal-sized pieces roughly the size of an egg. Working with one at a time, roll the pieces into ropes about ¾-inch wide. Cut the ropes into ¾-inch pieces.

PICK up one piece of the dough, roll it over the back of a fork or grooved gnocchi paddle, and let it drop onto the prepared baking sheet. Repeat with remaining pieces of dough. The resulting gnocchi should be slightly curved with grooves that will capture the sauce. Dust the gnocchi lightly with flour and set aside.

TO make the fonduta, place the cream in a medium saucepan. Cook over medium heat until the cream begins to simmer. Whisk in the 14-month Parmigiano Reggiano very gradually until it is all incorporated. Remove from the heat.

BRING a pot of water to a boil for the gnocchi. Meanwhile, melt the butter in a large sauté pan. When the water is boiling, salt it and add the gnocchi. Whisk ¼ cup of the gnocchi cooking water into the melted butter.

COOK the gnocchi until they rise to the top of the water, about 1 minute. As they are finished cooking, remove them with a slotted spoon and add to the pan with the butter. Sprinkle on the grated 18-month Parmigiano Reggiano and toss gently over medium heat until combined. Spoon a few tablespoons of the fonduta on each of 6 individual serving dishes. Top with gnocchi. Sprinkle the crumbled 36-month Parmigiano Reggiano on top and serve immediately.

FIRST THINGS FIRST

YOU'VE PROBABLY NOTICED BY NOW that our serving sizes for most recipes indicate how many people a pasta dish will serve as a first course. Pasta is one of Italy's many *primi*, or first-course dishes, which also include soups, polenta, rice dishes like risotto, and more. Traditionally, the midday meal in Italy consists of a first course, followed by a second course accompanied by side dishes or salads. On special occasions we eat dessert, but most days we finish lunch with a piece of fruit. This system probably developed as a canny way for people to fill up on less expensive pasta before turning to the pricier part of the meal. If you would rather serve pasta as the main course, figure four first-course portions will probably feed two to three people. A rich dish like these gnocchi may even satisfy five, especially if followed by a salad.

IL TOCCO FINALE

You've prepared a spectacular pasta dish and you're ready to serve it, but don't forget *il tocco finale*, "the finishing touch." Almost every pasta dish is topped with a flavorful ingredient. Look to what you used in the dish to make a good choice for the topping. Did you incorporate grated cheese in the pasta? Sprinkle a little more on top. Was the sauce made with olive oil? A drizzle of *olio crudo* will bring it all together. Do the textures call for some crunch? A dusting of breadcrumbs may be the answer.

BASILICO

Basil should be torn by hand rather than chopped and always added at the last minute, as it wilts on contact with heat. This herb pairs well with delicate spring vegetables, such as zucchini and asparagus.

OLIO PICCANTE

Spicy chile oil—popular in Calabria—is drizzled on a finished dish for zing. The oil gets spicier as it sits, so be sure not to go overboard, especially if you've had a jar in your cupboard for a while.

PREZZEMOLO

A handful of minced flat-leaf parsley adds a bright herbaceous flavor to almost any dish. It's best to pull the leaves off by hand before mincing.

GRANA PADANO A SCAGLIE

Grana Padano is another type of aged cheese in a large wheel. It comes from the Po Valley in northern Italy and is aged for at least one year. Like Parmigiano Reggiano, Grana Padano can be grated onto pasta, but it can also be shaved with a vegetable peeler. Sometimes these larger shavings provide a greater textural contrast to soft pasta.

PARMIGIANO REGGIANO GRATTUGIATO

Made in Parma, Reggio Emilia, Modena, Bologna (to the west of the Reno River), and Mantua (to the east of the Po River), this cheese is eaten almost everywhere in Italy. Note though that grated cheese is rarely paired with pasta dishes that contain fish or spicy sauces. If you are having dinner guests, pass around a grater and a hunk of cheese and let diners top their own pasta.

PANGRATTATO

As noted above, grated cheese is not served on pasta dishes with fish in Italy. Instead, we often use breadcrumbs as a topping for those dishes and others with flavors that might compete with subtle cheese. They add terrific crunch. Before using, simply toast them in a pan with a little olive oil until browned and fragrant. For an even bigger crunch, toast cubes of bread to create a crouton topping instead.

➤ *For the best breadcrumbs, trim the crust off stale bread, dry it out in a low oven, place it in a brown-paper bag, and crush it into irregular crumbs using a heavy skillet.*

OLIO D'OLIVA

A drizzle of olive oil is appropriate for just about any pasta dish with an olive oil sauce. (It will clash with butter sauces.) Try to find an oil from the region that is the home base of the dish you are making—the home team advantage of pasta cooking.

➤ *Remember olive oil is not just a carrier of other flavors; it imparts its own flavors to a dish, especially when used as a finishing touch on top. Next time you want to add a bit of bite at the end, instead of chile oil, try a spicy olive oil.*

GNOCCHI ALLA ROMANA
BAKED SEMOLINA GNOCCHI

Serves 10 as a first course

This rich primo gets any meal off to a festive start. It's particularly suited to the holidays because it can be prepared in advance and then popped in the oven at the last minute. If you have a set of small baking dishes, these can also be prepared as individual servings.

2 quarts whole milk

½ teaspoon freshly grated nutmeg

14 tablespoons (1 stick plus 6 tablespoons) unsalted butter

Fine sea salt to taste

3 cups semolina flour

4 large egg yolks

2½ cups grated Grana Padano cheese (see page 87)

BRUSH the top of a marble work surface or a large baking sheet with water and set aside.

PLACE the milk in a large saucepan with the nutmeg, 2 tablespoons of the butter, and salt and place over medium heat. As soon as the milk begins to bubble, slowly add the semolina, letting it trickle in while whisking constantly. If any lumps form, mash them against the side of the pot. When all the semolina has been added, continue to cook over medium heat, stirring constantly, until the mixture is very dense, 5 to 10 additional minutes. Remove from the heat and stir in the egg yolks, 2 tablespoons of the butter, and 1½ cups of the grated cheese. Work quickly and continue to stir until the semolina has cooled slightly. Taste and adjust salt if necessary.

TRANSFER the cooked semolina to the prepared work surface or baking sheet and with damp hands or an offset metal spatula that you moisten frequently, spread it evenly into a rectangle a little less than ½ inch thick. Allow the semolina to cool completely.

PREHEAT the oven to 400°F. Use 2 tablespoons of the butter to thickly grease a large rectangular baking dish (about 9 by 13 inches) and set aside.

USING a cookie cutter or the rim of a glass, cut out circles about 2 inches in diameter. Cut the circles side by side so that there are as few scraps as possible.

LIFT off the scraps from around the circles and place

them in the bottom of the dish, where they will be hidden. Dot with 4 tablespoons of the butter and sprinkle with ½ cup of the grated cheese.

ARRANGE the semolina circles in a single layer in the baking dish on top of the scraps, overlapping them (like shingles).

DOT the top with the remaining 4 tablespoons of butter and sprinkle on the remaining ½ cup grated cheese.

BAKE the gnocchi in the preheated oven until golden and crisp on top, 20 to 25 minutes. Allow to sit at room temperature for 10 minutes before serving.

GNUDI DI SPINACI E RICOTTA

SPINACH AND RICOTTA GNUDI WITH BUTTER SAUCE

Serves 6 as a first course

Gnudi are easy to make and impossible to dislike. The only slightly tricky part is shaping the mixture into quenelles, which are ovoid dumplings. If you prefer, you can roll the mixture into balls (about 2 tablespoons each) with lightly floured hands instead. Honestly, people gobble these up so quickly that no one will notice if they are slightly misshapen. Draining the ricotta well before you start makes the dough much easier to handle.

3 cups (about 1½ pounds) ricotta (see opposite)

1 cup 00 flour or unbleached all-purpose flour, plus more for dusting

1 pound spinach

½ cup grated Parmigiano Reggiano or Grana Padano, plus more for serving

2 large eggs, beaten

1 teaspoon fine sea salt

½ teaspoon freshly ground black pepper

Coarse sea salt for pasta cooking water

4 tablespoons (½ stick) unsalted butter, cut into cubes

PLACE the ricotta in a fine sieve set over a bowl to drain any excess liquid, cover the bowl with plastic wrap, and refrigerate it for at least 8 hours.

LINE a baking sheet with a lightly floured kitchen towel. Rinse the spinach and place the leaves in a large pot. Place over medium heat and let the spinach steam from the water that remains on the leaves, tossing occasionally, until it is wilted, about 5 minutes. When the spinach is cool enough to handle, squeeze it as dry as possible. Mince the spinach finely.

IN a medium bowl, combine the drained ricotta, ½ cup grated Parmigiano Reggiano or Grana Padano, spinach, 1 cup flour, eggs, fine sea salt, and pepper. Mix until a soft dough forms, gradually adding more flour in small amounts if the dough is sticky when poked.

DIP 2 soup spoons in cool water. Using one spoon, scoop up a heaping tablespoon of the ricotta mixture. Use the other spoon to form it into a quenelle. Repeat with the rest of the ricotta mixture. Once the gnudi are formed, gently toss them with flour so that they do not stick together. Place the gnudi on the prepared baking sheet.

BRING a large pot of water to a boil and season it with coarse sea salt. Gently slip as many of the gnudi at a time as will float freely in the pot. Stir gently with a wooden spoon. Cook until the gnudi rise to the surface (test for doneness by cutting into the center; the gnudi should be the same color and consistency all the way through). Scoop them out with a slotted spoon as soon as they are cooked, and transfer to a warm serving bowl. Repeat until all the gnudi are cooked.

WHILE the gnudi are cooking, place the butter in a sauté pan over medium heat and cook, watching carefully, until it smells toasty and the solids have turned a nutty brown. When all the gnudi are cooked, drizzle the browned butter over them, top with grated cheese, and serve immediately.

HOW TO MAKE RICOTTA

RICOTTA IS TECHNICALLY NOT A CHEESE—it is a by-product of the cheese-making process. This type of ricotta (created with milk rather than the whey used by large cheese-making operations) is easy to make at home. You can skip the heavy cream and make this with just milk if you like, but not skim milk—the resulting ricotta will be too grainy and watery. One gallon of milk will yield about 4 cups of ricotta.

1. Rinse out a large pot with cold water to prevent scorching. Place 1 gallon whole or reduced-fat milk or a combination of the two and ¾ to 1 cup heavy cream in the pot.

2. Heat, stirring occasionally, to somewhere between 185°F and 195°F, without bringing the milk mixture to a boil. If you don't have a thermometer, don't sweat it—just heat the milk until it is simmering actively but not boiling.

3. Remove from the heat and stir in ⅓ cup apple cider vinegar and 1 tablespoon fine sea salt. Stir constantly for 1 minute, then let the mixture cool untouched and uncovered for 10 minutes. Curds will form.

4. Line a fine-mesh sieve with damp cheesecloth and set the sieve over a bowl. Using a slotted spoon, transfer the ricotta to the lined strainer. (Pouring it will disturb the curd and may cause the bowl to overflow with liquid.) Refrigerate the ricotta until it has drained to the desired consistency—about 30 minutes for very smooth and creamy ricotta, or 2 to 3 hours for drier ricotta. Serve immediately or store in the refrigerator, in a covered container, for up to 5 days.

FILI D'ORO

When you knead eggs and flour into a dough, roll the dough out into a thin sheet, and then cut the sheet into strips of varying widths, you are doing more than just preparing pasta—you are participating in an age-old ritual that is still practiced daily in much of central and northern Italy.

Making your own egg pasta is fun, and it's not terribly difficult, but don't try to skip the step of allowing the pasta dough to rest before you roll it out by hand. After you've formed the dough, shape it into a ball and either wrap it or simply cover it with an overturned bowl (the goal is not to let it dry out as it rests) and set it aside on the work surface. You should also take this opportunity to scrape any bits of dried pasta dough off the surface so it's perfectly clean when you roll out the dough. Resting allows the dough to develop the proper elasticity—without a little "time out" it will crumble when you attempt to flatten it. Of course, if all this sounds daunting, you can always purchase fresh pasta at Eataly. We make it all day long.

GARGANELLI

Garganelli resemble penne and other tubular dried pasta, but they are made with egg pasta dough. To make garganelli, roll out the dough and cut it into squares (about 1½ inches per side). Wrap a square around a thin dowel (with the dowel crossing the square at two opposite corners) and then roll it on a wooden board with ridges like the teeth of a comb (see page 100) so that you simultaneously seal the square into a tube and create ridges on the outside of the pasta for capturing sauce.

TAGLIATELLE

Tagliatelle are ribbons of egg pasta cut about ¼ inch wide. For more about this pasta, which has a cult following in its native area in central Italy, see page 95.

➤ *The official width defined for tagliatelle is said to measure such that 12,270 pieces of the pasta stacked together would reach the height of the Torre degli Asinelli, one of Bologna's two famous towers.*

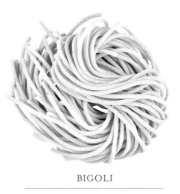

BIGOLI

Bigoli are long handmade pasta similar to spaghetti. While most fresh egg pasta is rolled out and cut, bigoli are extruded through a tool known as a torchio, or press. (Because of this, the dough for bigoli should be slightly drier than a dough that you plan to roll out.) Originating in the Veneto region, bigoli are typically served with a sauce of onion and anchovies (see page 130) or a rich walnut sauce. This sturdy pasta is often made with whole wheat flour, which gives them a rustic appeal.

CHITARRINE

Chitarrine, or spaghetti alla chitarra, are made using a tool that is strung like a guitar (see page 100). When viewed from the short end, they appear square in shape, and they generally incorporate semolina flour for extra chewiness. Chitarrine are a specialty in Abruzzo, but Romans make a very similar shape known as tonnarelli (see page 11).

TAGLIOLINI

Tagliolini are thin pasta strips, no more than 1/10 inch wide. They resemble fresh spaghetti and are also known as taglierini. (Taglio means "to cut" in Italian.)

TAGLIATELLE ALLA BOLOGNESE
TAGLIATELLE WITH BOLOGNESE RAGÙ

Serves 4 as a first course

A good ragù is a thing of beauty, but it is often misunderstood. Ragù is not a tomato sauce. Rather, it is a sauce of ground meat that is very lightly flavored with canned tomatoes or tomato paste. The predominant taste should be of the meat, and the meat should be cooked slowly—hurriedly browning it will dry it out. Ragù served over silken fresh egg tagliatelle is one of the signature dishes of the city of Bologna, and indeed this type of ragù is so closely associated with Bologna that any dish described as Bolognese, or Bologna style, will be cloaked in it.

2 tablespoons unsalted butter

2 tablespoons extra virgin olive oil

1 small yellow onion, minced

1 small carrot, minced

1 rib celery, minced

1 tablespoon minced garlic

4 ounces ground veal

4 ounces ground pork

4 ounces ground beef

Fine sea salt to taste

¼ cup white wine

¼ cup tomato paste

Freshly ground black pepper to taste

¼ cup chicken or beef stock

Coarse sea salt for pasta cooking water

IN a heavy Dutch oven or large heavy-bottomed pot over medium heat, melt the butter with the olive oil. Add the onion and cook, stirring frequently, until the onion is translucent, about 5 minutes. Add the carrot, celery, and garlic and cook, stirring frequently, until softened and fragrant, about 2 minutes more.

CRUMBLE the veal, pork, and beef into the pot. Season with fine sea salt. Reduce the heat to low and cook, stirring frequently, until the meat has rendered most of its fat and is just beginning to brown, about 5 minutes. Spoon out and discard some of the rendered fat, but leave enough to cover the bottom of the pan. (This will depend on the meat you're using—there may not be an excessive amount of fat.)

ADD the wine and increase the heat to medium. Cook, stirring occasionally, until the wine has evaporated, about 6 minutes.

DECREASE the heat to low, add the tomato paste, stir to combine, and cook, stirring frequently, for 20 minutes. Season to taste with salt and pepper. Add the stock and adjust the heat if necessary to reach a gentle simmer. Simmer until the stock has reduced but the sauce is still moist, about 45 minutes longer. Taste the sauce, adjust the seasoning if necessary, and remove from the heat.

Fresh tagliatelle made with approximately 4 cups unbleached all-purpose flour and 4 large eggs (see page 68)

Grated Grana Padano cheese (see page 87) for serving

BRING a large pot of water to a boil for the pasta. When the water is boiling, salt it with coarse salt (see page 22) and add the pasta. Cook until the pasta rises to the surface of the water (see page 22).

SMEAR a small amount of the sauce on the bottom of a warmed pasta serving bowl.

WHEN the pasta is cooked, drain it in a colander, then transfer it immediately to the serving bowl. Top with the remaining sauce and toss vigorously to combine. Serve immediately with grated cheese on the side.

AN EXALTED AND EXACT PASTA

ITALIANS ARE—WE CAN ADMIT IT—A LITTLE OBSESSED WITH FOOD. We talk about sfoglini and sfogline—the people who roll out *sfoglie,* or sheets, of egg pasta dough—almost as seriously and frequently as we discuss our favorite soccer players, especially in Emilia-Romagna, where egg pasta got its start. Certain food items develop a cult-like following in Italy, with official organizations that safeguard their reputation and dignity. One of those is the *tagliatella.*

A group called the Associazione Gli Apostoli della Tagliatella—literally the Association of Tagliatella Apostles—is headquartered in Bologna and is dedicated to all aspects of the art of making egg pasta. For its part, the Confraternità della Tagliatella recognizes restaurants that produce the finest egg pasta. These groups also have very strong opinions about a proper Bolognese ragù to pair with that pasta.

A tagliatella has specific measurements: a cooked piece should be 8 millimeters wide. This means an uncooked piece should be 6.5 to 7 millimeters when cut. (The thickness is a little less strictly regulated, but it should never exceed 1 millimeter.) In 1972, a single golden piece of pasta was produced as an example by the Bologna delegation to the Accademia Italiana della Cucina. It is housed in the offices of Bologna's chamber of commerce as a sign of the tagliatella's importance to the city.

TAJARIN CON BURRO AL TARTUFO
TAJARIN WITH TRUFFLE BUTTER

Serves 4 as a first course

Tajarin is the Piemontese dialect word for thin egg pasta strands known as taglierini elsewhere in Italy. You can make this with white truffles if you prefer.

Coarse sea salt for pasta cooking water

Fresh tajarin made with approximately 4 cups unbleached all-purpose flour, 2 whole eggs, and 4 egg yolks (see page 68)

1 tablespoon black truffle butter

Black truffle for shaving

BRING a large pot of water to a boil for the pasta. When the water is boiling, salt it (see page 22) and add the pasta. Cook until the pasta rises to the surface of the water, probably no more than 2 minutes (see page 22).

MEANWHILE, heat the truffle butter over very low heat in a saucepan large enough to hold the pasta. Remove from the heat as soon as the butter is melted.

DRAIN the pasta, reserving about 1 cup cooking water, and add the pasta to the pan with the truffle butter. Toss over high heat to coat the pasta. Add small amounts of pasta cooking water, if necessary, to keep the sauce from getting too dense. Divide equally among 4 heated pasta bowls, shave black truffle over the top, and serve immediately.

FETTUCCINE ALLA MARCHIGIANA
MARCHE-STYLE FETTUCCINE

Serves 2 as a first course

Situated in the center of the country on the Adriatic Sea, the Marche is known for its excellent pork products, sheep's cheese, and wheat. It is a hub for organic farming in Italy: at last count, more than 12 percent of the farmland in the region was cultivated using organic methods.

2 tablespoons extra virgin olive oil

2 ounces guanciale (cured pork jowl), cut into batons

1 small red onion, halved and sliced

1 clove garlic, sliced

Fine sea salt to taste

Coarse sea salt for pasta cooking water

Fettuccine made with 2 eggs and 2 cups farro flour (see page 68)

½ cup grated aged Pecorino cheese

PLACE the olive oil and guanciale in a sauté pan over medium-high heat. Add the onion, garlic, and a pinch of fine sea salt and cook until the guanciale is slightly browned. Remove the pan from the heat and set aside.

BRING a large pot of water to a boil over high heat and season with coarse sea salt (see page 22). Add the fettuccine to the water and cook until it rises to the surface, about 2 minutes (see page 22). Remove the pasta from the water (reserve cooking water) and add it to the pan with the guanciale and onion. Toss over medium heat (using 2 large forks can be helpful) to evenly coat the pasta with the sauce. Remove the pasta from the heat.

SPRINKLE in the Pecorino and a bit of cooking water if the pasta seems too dry. Toss to combine and serve immediately.

PAPPARDELLE AL SUGO DI CONIGLIO

PAPPARDELLE WITH RABBIT SAUCE

Serves 6 as a first course

This pasta recipe brings the somewhat subtle taste of rabbit to the fore. Rabbit is relatively lean, so it should be cooked for a long time at a low temperature.

1 rabbit (about 2 pounds), cut up

Fine sea salt to taste

¼ cup extra virgin olive oil

2 carrots

2 leeks

½ cup chicken stock

¼ cup tomato puree

Fresh pappardelle made with approximately 6 cups unbleached all-purpose flour and 6 large eggs (see page 68)

Coarse sea salt for pasta cooking water

1 tablespoon unsalted butter

¼ cup grated Parmigiano Reggiano

PREHEAT the oven to 200°F.

SEASON the rabbit generously with salt and place in a roasting pan large enough to fit the pieces in a single layer. Heat the olive oil until warm and pour it over the rabbit. Roast until tender and browned, about 2 hours.

MEANWHILE, dice the carrots and the white part of the leeks. Bring a small pot of water to a boil, add the vegetables, and cook until the carrots are soft, about 8 minutes. Drain and reserve.

BRING a large pot of water to a boil for cooking the pasta.

WHEN the rabbit is cooked (an instant-read thermometer registers an internal temperature of 160°F) and cool enough to handle, remove the meat from the bone. (You can pull it off with your fingers—you want it to be in pieces.) Discard the bones or save for use in a stock.

PLACE a large skillet over medium heat. Add the cooked carrots, leeks, chicken stock, and tomato puree, and stir to combine. Season with salt and simmer over low heat while preparing the pasta.

MEANWHILE, when the water boils, add salt (see page 22), and then add the pappardelle. Cook, stirring frequently with a long-handled fork, until the pappardelle rise to the top and are cooked al dente (see page 22).

ADD the rabbit meat to the simmering sauce and cook until heated through. When the pasta is cooked, drop the butter into the pan with the sauce and stir it in. Drain the pasta in a colander. Transfer the pasta to the pan with the sauce. Toss vigorously over medium heat until combined, about 2 minutes. Remove from heat and stir in the cheese. Serve immediately.

ATTREZZI PER FARE LA PASTA

Pasta making is not a high-tech art. Even hand-crank pasta machines are rarely used in Italy, as the metal rollers produce a slicker surface than you get if you roll out the dough with a wooden rolling pin on a wooden surface. That said, there are a few *attrezzi* that can make your life in the pasta kitchen easier, and a few you cannot do without. As with everything, having the right tool for the job is key.

CHITARRA

If you want to make true spaghetti alla chitarra or chitarrine, you'll need this special tool. A sfoglia, or "sheet," of pasta is placed on top, and then you roll over it with a rolling pin as the evenly sized pasta strips collect in the box below.

MATTARELLO

The rolling pin for making pasta is a dowel-style wooden rolling pin (not the type with the handles that roll independently of the body). It is useful to have a board with a lip on it that hooks over the side of the counter to use as a work surface as well.

SPINETTE E SPIEDINI

Some types of pasta are formed by being wrapped around thin wooden dowels (spinette) and metal skewers (spiedini) to form tubes or spirals. Keep a few different sizes on hand so you have options. A knitting needle will do in a pinch—typical Italian ingenuity. Never press the pasta too firmly against the dowel or skewer when shaping or it will stick. Use a light hand so the finished pasta will slide off easily.

ROTELLE

You can cut individual pieces of pasta such as ravioli with a knife, but you'll get prettier results with a wheel cutter (two types are shown opposite). You can use a straight-edge wheel cutter for larger pieces, or choose a fluted or serrated cutter for smaller shapes. The cutter helps to seal the two edges a little as it separates the pieces from each other.

TAGLIERINO RIGA

Sometimes called a pettina, or "comb," this board is used to create ridges on gnocchi, garganelli, and a few other types of pasta.

TAGLIA RAVIOLI

You can make plain ravioli by dotting a strip of egg pasta with filling, placing another layer of pasta on top, and sealing the two sheets together, then cutting the ravioli with a knife. But using a ravioli stamp, which is similar to a cookie cutter, you'll obtain prettier results.

chitarra

spinette

taglia ravioli

mattarello

rotelle

spiedini

taglierino riga

CHITARRINE CON TERRA E MARE

"SURF AND TURF" CHITARRA PASTA

Serves 4 as a first course

Terra e mare literally means "land and sea"—the Italian version of "surf and turf." It refers to any dish that combines seafood with meat or mushrooms or other items found inland. 'Nduja is a spicy pork salami from Calabria that is soft and spreadable.

2 tablespoons extra virgin olive oil

2 cloves garlic

8 ounces shrimp, peeled, deveined and cut into bite-size pieces

Fine sea salt to taste

Coarse sea salt for cooking pasta

1½ pounds squid ink chitarrine (see note below)

¼ cup diced 'nduja, casing removed

2 tablespoons white wine

2 teaspoons crushed red pepper flakes

¾ cup tomato puree

¼ cup chopped flat-leaf parsley

BRING 6 quarts of water to a boil for the pasta. Meanwhile, heat a sauté pan over low heat. Once the pan is warm, add the oil and garlic cloves. Cook, stirring frequently, until the garlic is browned, then remove and discard it. Add the shrimp and sauté until cooked through. Season with fine sea salt and remove from the pan with a slotted spoon and set aside.

SEASON the boiling water with coarse sea salt (see page 22) and add the pasta.

ADD the 'nduja to the pan in which you cooked the shrimp and turn the heat up to medium high. Deglaze the pan with the wine. Add the red pepper flakes and cook, stirring frequently, until the wine has reduced by three-quarters. Add the tomato puree and continue to cook until the sauce has reduced by about a quarter and is thickened. Taste and adjust salt.

WHEN the pasta is al dente (see page 22), scoop out 1 cup of the cooking water and set aside. Drain the pasta in a colander, then transfer to the pan with the sauce.

TOSS the pasta vigorously to coat it with the sauce. Add the shrimp and parsley and continue to toss with the sauce. If the sauce is too thick, add some cooking water in small amounts. Toss to combine well and serve immediately.

NOTE: You can purchase squid ink chitarrine at Eataly. But if you'd like to make your own, start with the directions on pages 68–69, making the dough with 4 large eggs and 4 cups 00 flour or unbleached all-purpose flour. Add squid ink to the flour well with the eggs in step 1 and proceed. Use about 1 tablespoon squid ink per egg/portion. Roll out the dough and lay a sheet atop a chitarra (page 100), then use a rolling pin to press the dough through the strings, creating square-shaped pasta.

SPAGHETTI ALLA CHITARRA CON ZUCCHINE E ACCIUGHE SALATE

CHITARRA PASTA WITH ZUCCHINI AND ANCHOVIES

Serves 4 to 6 as a first course

This pretty dish is a good choice for spring. Of course, you can toss the puree and the pasta together if you like, but composing the dish with a pool of puree on the bottom is more elegant.

4 pounds zucchini

5 tablespoons unsalted butter

1 yellow onion, thinly sliced

1 cup tightly packed fresh spinach

3 salted anchovy fillets, rinsed

Coarse sea salt for pasta cooking water

Spaghetti alla chitarra made with 4 large eggs and 4 cups 00 flour or unbleached all-purpose flour (see page 68 for dough and page 103 for cutting instructions)

CUT 3 pounds of the zucchini into large chunks. In a medium skillet melt 1 tablespoon of the butter over medium heat. Add the zucchini chunks and onion and cook until soft. Transfer the mixture to a blender and blend until smooth. Add the spinach and blend again until it is completely pureed and combined. Set aside.

CUT the remaining 1 pound zucchini into thin strips. Salt lightly and place in a sieve to drain for 10 to 15 minutes. Rinse and pat dry.

MELT 1 tablespoon of the remaining butter in a skillet, add the anchovy fillets, and cook, stirring frequently, until the anchovies dissolve. Add the zucchini strips and cook over low heat until softened; do not brown.

MEANWHILE, bring a large pot of water to a boil for the pasta and season with coarse salt (see page 22). Add the pasta to the water and cook until it floats to the top. Transfer the pasta to the skillet, reserving cooking water. Add about 3 tablespoons of the reserved cooking water to the skillet, along with the remaining 3 tablespoons butter, and cook, tossing, until combined. Add small amounts of additional cooking water if the pan seems dry.

TO serve, place about ¼ cup of the zucchini puree in the base of each individual serving plate. Twist portions of the pasta into a nest and place on top.

MALTAGLIATI CON FUNGHI

MALTAGLIATI WITH MUSHROOMS

Serves 4 as a first course

Maltagliati means "badly cut," and this pasta is meant to be somewhat irregular in shape. Cut the dough into diamonds, triangles, and rectangles that are roughly 2 by 3 inches.

6 large button mushrooms

6 shiitake mushrooms

6 oyster mushrooms

5 tablespoons extra virgin olive oil

2 cloves garlic, crushed

Fine sea salt and freshly ground black pepper to taste

1 medium shallot, minced

2 sprigs fresh thyme

Coarse sea salt for pasta cooking water

Maltagliati (see note above) made with 4 cups 00 flour or unbleached all-purpose flour and 4 large eggs (see page 68)

1 tablespoon unsalted butter

2 tablespoons fresh flat-leaf chopped parsley

½ cup grated Parmigiano Reggiano or Grana Padano

SLICE all the mushrooms about ¼-inch thick.

HEAT a large heavy-bottomed pan over medium-high heat until very hot. Place 3 tablespoons of the olive oil and the garlic in the pan. Toast the garlic until brown and then remove and discard. Add the mushrooms and season with salt and pepper. Let cook 1 minute and then add the shallot and thyme and cook, stirring, until the mushrooms have given up their liquid and begin to brown, 3 to 4 minutes. Remove the pan from the heat, discard the thyme, and set aside.

BRING a large pot of water to a boil for the pasta and season with coarse salt (see page 22). Return the pan with the mushrooms to medium heat. After you have added the pasta to the cooking water, remove about ¼ cup pasta cooking water and add it to the pan with the mushrooms. Add the butter to the pan with the mushrooms as well.

WHEN the pasta rises to the surface, about 3 minutes, transfer it (reserving cooking water) to the pan with the mushrooms. Toss vigorously over medium heat for 1 minute. Add a little more pasta cooking water if the pan looks dry. Remove from the heat and stir in the remaining 2 tablespoons of olive oil, the parsley, and grated cheese. Taste and adjust seasoning if necessary, then serve immediately.

UNA PASSIONE SELVATICA

Italy was a heavily agricultural country for many years, and we Italians are still in close touch with the land. Even in big cities, you'll see apartment terraces where people tend to a few potted tomato plants and flowers. And we always enjoy heading into the woods to forage for wild ingredients. Field greens and other foraged items are sold at farmer's markets, and sometimes foragers who have found more than they can use simply stand by the side of the road and sell bunches of greens and baskets of mushrooms. It's all part of the Italian commitment to eating locally, known as *kilometro zero*. At Eataly, too, we love sharing local products, and we think the freshest ingredients always taste best.

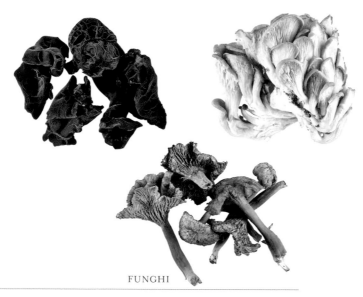

FUNGHI

Meaty porcini mushrooms—available in early fall—are one of the biggest scores, but Italian forests are home to a mother lode of various kinds of mushrooms, from chiodini mushrooms to finferli (chanterelles) to ovoli (which, as their name implies, look like eggs). We also love oyster mushrooms, whose meaty flavor makes them a good substitute for portobello and cremini mushrooms, and wood ear mushrooms, which have a pleasantly chewy texture. Be sure to consult a knowledgeable mycologist before eating any mushroom you find in the wild. Poisonous and nonpoisonous varieties can bear a striking resemblance to one another.

➤ *The porcini of Borgotaro, found in Emilia-Romagna, have IGP (Protected Geographic Indication) status, a high honor.*

TARTUFI NERI

Black truffles, found in the Norcia area of Umbria, are slightly less refined than white truffles but still an extraordinary fungus that elevates almost any dish. Their dark skin is bumpy, and the interior of a black truffle is grayish brown and riddled with veins. Unlike their white cousins, black truffles can be heated briefly. Black truffles grow amid oak and hazelnut trees and are harvested in late autumn and winter.

Black summer truffles, sometimes called scorzone, look like their fall/winter counterparts, though their skin is thicker. They also have a lighter, sweeter flavor, and that less forceful personality pairs well with spring and summer dishes.

➤ Black truffles taste like soil, in the best possible way, and they have an aftertaste similar to cocoa or unsweetened chocolate.

AGLIO ORSINO

Aglio orsino, commonly known as ramps in English, are a kind of wild garlic, but rather than using the bulb, you eat the plant's sharply flavored green leaves. Aglio orsino is sometimes pickled so that it can be enjoyed over the winter. It has a short season in early spring.

ASPARAGI SELVATICI

Wild asparagus is pencil-thin and grows in the spring in sandy soil and sometimes amid thorny bushes, so exercise caution! Always cut asparagus rather than pulling it out by the root, so it will continue to flourish.

TARTUFI BIANCHI

Revered as the ultimate culinary indulgence, fresh Italian white truffles from Piemonte are available for only a few months each year in the fall. White truffles aren't really white—they're more of a creamy beige color with a smooth surface. And they smell funky, like a mushroom cranked up a few notches, perhaps with a splash of dark honey. During the annual Fiera Internazionale del Tartufo Bianco d'Alba, the air is so perfumed with their scent that you can practically experience a contact truffle high! Truffles are expensive, but a little goes a long way. White truffles are never cooked. They are simply shaved into thin petals over cooked foods. (You'll want a dedicated truffle slicer so no other aromas intrude.) White truffles must be eaten within a week of being dug up from the forest floor.

➤ Truffle hunters don't use pigs anymore because the animals would clamp their powerful jaws onto the truffles and refuse to give them up. Nowadays dogs are much preferred since they're good at finding the truffles but don't have a taste for eating them.

ORTICA

Stinging nettles, available in the spring, are covered in little prickers, so be sure to wear protective gloves if you head out in search of them and when handling them back in your kitchen. Once cooked they are harmless—not to mention astringent and delicious. They grow in damp areas.

LASAGNE PRIMAVERA
LASAGNE WITH SPRING VEGETABLES

Serves 6 as a first course

Traditional Bolognese lasagne (note that *lasagne* is the plural form of the pasta, a *lasagna* would be a single wide strip of pasta—not a very satisfying portion!) is made with béchamel and Bolognese ragù (page 94), but there are lots of interesting variations on baked pasta that you can make with fresh egg pasta once you've got the hang of them. This dish is popular in spring, but you can swap different seasonal vegetables for the asparagus and peas. If you are using fresh peas and shelling them yourself, you will need approximately ¾ pound.

2 cups whole milk

1 bay leaf

4 to 5 whole black peppercorns

4 tablespoons (½ stick) unsalted butter

3 tablespoons unbleached all-purpose flour

Fine sea salt to taste

Pinch freshly grated nutmeg

1 clove garlic

Leaves of 1 bunch fresh basil (about 2 loosely packed cups)

2 tablespoons pine nuts, plus more for garnish

½ cup extra virgin olive oil, plus more for oiling pan

¾ cup grated Pecorino Romano

About 24 fresh 4-by-10-inch egg pasta lasagne made with about 3 cups unbleached all-purpose flour and 3 large eggs (see page 68)

Coarse sea salt for pasta cooking water

1 pound asparagus, cut in half lengthwise if thick

1 cup fresh shelled or frozen peas

PLACE the milk in a small saucepan with the bay leaf and the peppercorns and warm over low heat. Strain out and discard the bay leaf and peppercorns. In another small saucepan, melt the butter. Whisk in the flour and cook, whisking constantly, over low heat for 2 minutes. Add the warm milk 2 tablespoons at a time, stirring to combine between additions. Add fine sea salt to taste and cook, stirring, until the mixture has the consistency of sour cream and has no hint of raw-flour flavor, about 15 minutes. Stir in the nutmeg and set aside.

PLACE the garlic and a generous pinch of fine sea salt in a large mortar and grind against the sides until crushed into a paste. Reserve a few basil leaves for garnish, and add about a quarter of the remaining basil leaves to the mortar and grind until broken down. Continue to add the basil a little at a time, breaking down all the leaves before adding more. Add the 2 tablespoons pine nuts and grind until crushed. Add the oil and grind until the pesto is creamy. Finally, add ½ cup of the Pecorino Romano cheese and grind until creamy and thoroughly combined.

BRING a large pot of water to a boil for cooking the pasta. Spread a clean flat-weave dish towel on a work surface and set a bowl of ice water nearby. When the water is boiling, salt it with the coarse salt (see page 22) and add 4 of the pasta sheets. Cook until the pasta rises to the surface, about 30 seconds (see page 22), then

109

remove with a skimmer, dip briefly in the cold water, and spread on the dish towel in a single layer. Repeat with the remaining pasta. Gently blot the pasta dry.

PLACE the asparagus in a skillet in one layer. Add water just to cover, salt, and simmer over medium heat until just tender, 3 to 5 minutes. Remove with a slotted spoon, shock in ice water, drain, and chop into ½-inch lengths. Meanwhile, add the peas to the same skillet. Add a little more water to cover if necessary and simmer over medium heat until just tender, 5 minutes for fresh peas, less for frozen peas. Drain and set aside.

PREHEAT the oven to 450°F. Lightly oil a 13-by-9-inch baking pan. Divide the béchamel loosely into fifths and the pesto loosely into quarters (no need to be exact). Cover the bottom of the pan with a layer of pasta, cutting them to fit if necessary. (You will make 9 layers of lasagne pasta in all, but this is the only layer that should fit tightly in the pan. With the rest, you have more leeway.) Spread about one-fifth of the béchamel on top of the pasta. Top with another layer of pasta. Spread about one-quarter of the pesto on top of the pasta, then one-fifth of the béchamel. Sprinkle on 2 tablespoons of grated Pecorino Romano. Sprinkle about one-third of the chopped asparagus and peas in an even layer. Top the vegetables with one-fifth of the béchamel, then another layer of pasta.

CONTINUE assembling by topping the layer of pasta with one-quarter of the pesto, another layer of pasta, and another one-third of the vegetables. Add another layer of pasta, another one-quarter of the pesto, another layer of pasta, and the remaining vegetables. Top these with another layer of pasta, the remaining pesto, another layer of pasta, one-fifth of the béchamel, and the remaining pasta. Spread the remaining béchamel on top, sprinkle on the remaining 2 tablespoons of Pecorino Romano, and bake until a crust forms and the top is browned, about 10 minutes. If the top has not browned after 10 minutes, place under the broiler until it does, about 4 minutes.

HOW TO MAKE BESCIAMELLA

DON'T BE FOOLED BY THAT FRENCH NAME—béchamel is an Italian invention! (The proper Italian name is *besciamella* or *balsamella*.) It's a simple white sauce made with butter, flour, and milk. It's often used as a binder in pasta dishes, especially baked dishes that would risk getting dried out in the oven without its assistance.

Béchamel can be made in varying degrees of thickness depending on the amount of flour incorporated and the length of cooking. The process is always the same: For about 2 cups of besciamella, first melt 3 tablespoons butter in a pot with a heavy bottom. Do not brown the butter. Add ¼ cup sifted 00 flour or unbleached all-purpose flour and whisk over low heat for 2 minutes. Again, you do not want it to brown. You're not making a roux; you simply want to eliminate the raw flavor of the flour.

Add 2 cups scalded milk in a very thin stream (stopping and starting if necessary to incorporate between additions) while whisking constantly. Continue cooking and whisking until the béchamel has reached the desired thickness—you can bring the consistency anywhere from heavy cream to strained yogurt. Even the thickest béchamel should be ready in 15 minutes. If lumps do form, don't despair—you can always strain your béchamel to remove them.

Salt béchamel lightly at the end of cooking. Depending on how you'll be using it, you may also want to add a grinding of pepper and/or a grating of nutmeg. Béchamel can be made in advance and refrigerated, but it will not spread when cold, so reheat it gently before using it.

Strati di Gloria

FIRST, A LINGUISTIC CLARIFICATION: a *lasagna* is a single large strip of pasta. A dish of many of these strips is known as *lasagne*.

Lasagne is a complex dish with many components, but every single one of them can be made in advance. Additionally, cutting large rectangular strips is easy: you simply place a sheet of pasta on a work surface and cut them with a knife or wheel cutter. In short, don't be intimidated by lasagne. It is not difficult to make; you're just not going to be able to throw it together on the spur of the moment.

Pasta for lasagne is made with standard egg dough, or with spinach dough. While you don't want the strips to be overly thick, the sheet of dough can be a little less thin than you would typically aim for with other shapes, as once the lasagne are cooked and layered you won't be able to assess the thickness of each individual piece.

Lasagne are usually rectangles about 4 by 10 inches, but keep your pan size and shape in mind when cutting them. Once they're cooked, cover the bottom of a lightly oiled or buttered baking pan (you can also smear it with a bit of ragù if you're making a traditional lasagne) with a single layer of the pasta. The strips should overlap slightly but not too much, and never let the edges of the pasta rest vertically against the sides of the pan—they'll dry out and be inedible. Trim small pieces to fill any gaps.

Use ingredients sparingly. Lasagne is not an overstuffed, everything-but-the-kitchen-sink casserole. It is a balanced dish. Choose your pan size so that you don't have more than 6 layers of pasta (except for in the vincisgrassi on page 114, which traditionally have 7 layers or more), and be sure it's deep enough that the final layer is at least ½ inch from the top of the pan. The easiest way to add béchamel is to drop small amounts on the lasagne with a spoon, then use the back of the spoon to spread it evenly.

Ragù should be used just as sparingly. The layer of sauce should be thin enough that you can see the pasta underneath, and bits of meat in the sauce should be scattered across the surface rather than thickly coating it.

No matter how many layers you produce, lasagne always ends with a layer of sauce, and then a sprinkling of grated cheese. The cheese browns in the oven, creating an attractive crust.

Use a sharp knife to slice the pasta sheets to fit the pan.

Spread an even layer of besciamella sauce using the back of a spoon.

In traditional lasagne, we use a grated aged cheese such as Parmigiano Reggiano, not mozzarella.

VINCISGRASSI

RICH VEAL AND CHICKEN LIVER LASAGNE

Serves 6 to 8 as a first course

If you don't have veal stock on hand, buy your veal on the bone and use the bones to make stock, reserving the meat for the sauce. Sometimes porcini mushrooms are incorporated into this dish.

6 ounces chicken livers

¼ cup extra virgin olive oil

1½ pounds veal shoulder, chopped

1 yellow onion

3 to 4 whole cloves

Fine sea salt and freshly ground black pepper to taste

1 carrot, minced

2 ribs celery, minced

½ cup dry white wine

2 cups canned peeled tomatoes, chopped

2 cups veal stock

9 tablespoons (1 stick plus 1 tablespoon) unsalted butter

½ cup 00 flour or unbleached all-purpose flour

4 cups whole milk, scalded

Coarse sea salt for pasta cooking water

About 48 fresh 4-by-10-inch egg pasta strips made with approximately 6 cups 00 flour or unbleached all-purpose flour and 6 large eggs (see page 68)

1 cup grated Parmigiano Reggiano

IN a small skillet, sauté the chicken livers in 2 tablespoons of the olive oil until browned. Mince and set aside. Heat the remaining 2 tablespoons olive oil in a heavy pot and cook the veal until it no longer looks raw. Stud the onion with the cloves. Season the veal with salt and pepper and add the carrot, celery, and onion. Brown for a few minutes, then add the wine and deglaze the pot. When the wine has evaporated, add the chicken livers, chopped tomatoes, and the stock. Simmer gently over low heat for at least 1½ hours, adding small amounts of water if the sauce seems to be getting overly dense.

WHEN the sauce is cooked, preheat the oven to 350°F. Thickly butter a 13-by-9-inch baking pan with about 2 tablespoons of the butter and set aside.

MAKE a béchamel. Melt 5 tablespoons of the remaining butter in a pot. Whisk in the flour and cook for 2 minutes. Add the milk in a thin stream, whisking constantly, and cook until the sauce has the consistency of sour cream. Remove from the heat and season lightly with salt.

BRING a large pot of water to a boil for cooking the pasta. Season with coarse salt and cook the pasta until just al dente (see page 22). Spread the pasta in a single layer on kitchen towels and blot to dry.

LINE the bottom of the prepared pan with pasta strips, overlapping slightly. (See pages 112–113.) Spread a layer of meat sauce, then béchamel, and then sprinkle with some of the grated cheese. Continue to make layers in this fashion, ending with a layer of sauce and grated cheese on top. Dot with the remaining 2 tablespoons butter. Bake until bubbling and browned, about 45 minutes. Let the dish rest for 10 minutes before serving.

MLINCI CON POLLO IN UMIDO

ROASTED EGG PASTA WITH CHICKEN STEW

Serves 4 as a main course

Friuli Venezia Giulia in the northeastern corner of Italy borders Austria and Slovenia, and mlinci strongly reflect the influence of those neighbors. This egg pasta is rolled into a sheet, then toasted briefly in the oven before being cooked. It is often paired with poultry; in addition to chicken, mlinci are often served with goose or duck. Sometimes minced herbs are incorporated into the pasta dough.

¼ cup plus 2 tablespoons extra virgin olive oil

1 whole chicken, cut up

1 yellow onion, diced

2 carrots, diced

1 cup white wine

Fine sea salt and freshly ground pepper to taste

About 3 cups chicken broth (see page 74)

4 cups 00 flour or unbleached all-purpose flour, plus more for flouring pans

4 large eggs

Coarse sea salt for pasta cooking water

HEAT 2 tablespoons of the olive oil in a large Dutch oven over medium heat and brown the chicken on all sides. Add the onion and carrots and cook until the onion begins to brown, then add the wine to the pot and scrape up any bits that have stuck to the bottom. Season with salt and pepper and cook at a brisk simmer until the wine has reduced by half. Add the broth. The broth should cover the chicken. If it doesn't, add more broth or a little water. Reduce the heat to low and simmer until the chicken is cooked through and the meat is falling off the bones, about 2 hours.

PREHEAT the oven to 400°F. Flour 2 baking sheets and set aside.

MAKE a pasta dough with the 4 cups flour, eggs, and the remaining ¼ cup olive oil. (See page 68). Roll into thin sheets. Place the pasta sheets on the prepared pans and roast in the oven until the sheets are dotted with brown spots and smell toasty, 10 to 15 minutes. Break the sheets of dough into pieces with your hands. (They are meant to be irregular in size and shape.)

WHEN the chicken is cooked, strip the meat from the bones. Discard bones and skin and return the meat to the pot. Bring a large pot of water to a boil, season with coarse salt (see page 22), and add the mlinci. Cook until tender, about 5 minutes. Remove the mlinci with a slotted spoon or skimmer and transfer them to the pot with the chicken. Stir to combine and serve hot.

FARINA + ACQUA = MAGIA

Nowhere is Italian culinary ingenuity more in evidence than in the simplest of homemade pastas: eggless pastas crafted out of nothing more than flour and water. Many use semolina flour for extra chewiness. The southern regions of Italy—historically the less wealthy part of the country where even eggs were once a luxury—are particularly fertile ground for this type of pasta, known as *maccheroni*.

Without egg incorporated for elasticity, flour-and-water pasta dough is a little sturdier. It requires a few minutes more kneading time than egg pasta dough does, and it will be a pale beige color rather than yellow. Also, flour-and-water dough isn't rolled into a thin sheet, or *sfoglia*, like egg pasta. See individual recipes for instructions on shaping pasta and see page 128 for more information on semolina flour.

MALLOREDDUS

The name is believed to come from the Sardo dialect word for "bull." It may be because these resemble fattened calves. Others believe it is because Sardinian cooks had a habit of making larger pasta shapes first and then using leftover bits of dough to form these shapes, which are sometimes as small as a thumbnail. Thus they were the little calves that came from the rest of the dough. They are also known as gnocchetti sardi, *or "little Sardinian dumplings."*

BUSIATE

*Trapani in western Sicilia is the source of these long pasta spirals. In old times they were made by wrapping the dough around reeds (*busa*) but in modern times knitting needles are used.*

CAVATELLI

Cavatelli are southern semolina-flour pasta shaped like hot dog buns—hence the name, which indicates that they are hollow (cavati) inside. Some use the serrated edge of a butter knife to create extra ridges when flattening and rolling the pieces. It's all about creating multiple opportunities for sauce to cling to the pasta.

ORECCHIETTE

These "little ears" made of semolina flour and water are the pride of the Puglia region. The trick in making these is to drag the pieces out while simultaneously thinning them with a fingertip, preferably a thumb. This action, especially when done atop a wooden board that has a bit of raised grain to it, is what gives orecchiette their irresistible wrinkles.

PICI

Created by Sienese pastai—"pasta makers"— pici are thick strands of pasta made with a simple dough of flour and water that is cut into strips and then hand-rolled. In some parts of Toscana, semolina flour is incorporated; a similar pasta in Umbria often incorporates a little farro flour. The name means "tiny."

STRASCINATI

Strascinati are curled pasta pieces similar to orecchiette—and also from Puglia—that are made by dragging (the name means "dragged ones") each individual piece across the work surface to thin it. This gives them a raised border that's thicker and chewier and a thinner middle. They are relatively easy to shape and a good project for beginning pasta makers.

ORECCHIETTE CON CIME
DI RAPA E PECORINO

ORECCHIETTE WITH BROCCOLI RABE AND PECORINO

Serves 4 as a first course

Puglia's signature pasta, orecchiette, is wonderfully chewy due to a healthy dose of harder semolina flour. Orecchiette are shaped by being dragged across a wooden work surface rather than being rolled out, so the dough does not need to rest before shaping. Because orecchiette contain no egg, they keep very well. You can prepare orecchiette and let them dry completely on the baking sheets, then store them in tightly sealed jars or other containers for up to two months, or you can use them immediately. In the latter case, they will cook quickly. You can substitute packaged orecchiette in this recipe, but because orecchiette are relatively simple to produce at home and can be stored at length, you owe it to yourself to try making them at least once.

1 cup durum semolina flour

1½ cups unbleached all-purpose flour, plus more for flouring work surface and hands

Coarse sea salt for cooking water

1 bunch broccoli rabe, any fibrous stems trimmed

¼ cup extra virgin olive oil, plus more for drizzling

1 clove garlic

¼ cup grated aged Pecorino, preferably from Puglia

Crushed red pepper flakes to taste

IN a medium bowl, use a whisk to combine the two flours completely. Mound the flour on a work surface and make a well in the center.

PLACE about 2 tablespoons room-temperature (not cold) water in the well. With two fingers, stir in some of the flour off the walls and into the center. When the water has been absorbed, repeat with more water, always adding small amounts, until you have a soft dough. (You will probably need between ⅔ cup and 1 cup water. If necessary, reshape the mound of flour between additions.)

KNEAD the dough until it is smooth and soft, about 10 minutes. If it crumbles while you are kneading, wet your hands a few times to incorporate a small amount of additional liquid.

LIGHTLY flour a baking sheet and set aside. Cut off a piece of dough about the size of a golf ball and put the remaining dough under an overturned bowl to keep it from drying out. On the work surface, roll the piece of dough into a rope about ½ inch wide.

(continued)

USE a knife to slice off a disk about 1⅛ inch wide and pull the disk away from the rope of dough, pressing it against the work surface. Then lift up the disk and invert it over a fingertip. It should be shaped like a little hat with a rolled "brim" all around the perimeter. Transfer the shaped pasta to the prepared baking sheet. Repeat with the remaining rope of dough, then with the remaining pasta dough.

BRING a large pot of water to a boil. When the water boils, add salt and cook the broccoli rabe until tender, 3 to 5 minutes.

REMOVE the broccoli rabe with a slotted spoon and run under cold water. Squeeze as much water as possible out of the broccoli rabe and chop roughly. Set aside.

LET the water return to a boil, then add the orecchiette and cook until al dente, about 5 minutes if freshly made and 12 minutes for orecchiette that you have made and allowed to dry completely (the time will vary depending on how dry the pasta dough is and how thick or thin it is). Taste a few pieces to account for variation.

HEAT 2 tablespoons oil in a large pan. Peel and crush the garlic clove, sauté it until browned, then remove it from the pan with a slotted spoon and discard.

WHEN the pasta is cooked, drain it and add it to the pan along with the remaining olive oil and the chopped broccoli rabe. Toss over medium heat until combined, about 2 minutes. Remove the pan from the heat, sprinkle on the grated cheese and some red pepper flakes, and toss to combine. Finish with a drizzle of olive oil and serve immediately.

PICI ALL'AGLIONE

PICI WITH GARLICKY SAUCE

Serves 6 as a first course

Pici pair well with a variety of sauces, from smooth tomato sauce to hearty meat ragu. *Aglione* means "big garlic," and you can increase the amount here even further if you're a fan!

4 cups 00 flour or unbleached all-purpose flour

¼ cup extra virgin olive oil

4 to 6 cloves garlic, minced

1 pinch red pepper flakes (optional)

1 (28-ounce) can whole peeled tomatoes, crushed

Fine sea salt and freshly ground black pepper to taste

Coarse sea salt for pasta cooking water

Leaves of 3 sprigs fresh basil, torn

TO make the pasta, place the flour in a bowl and add about 1 cup warm water. Stir with a fork to combine. Continue adding water in small amounts until you have a soft dough. You will probably need between 1¼ and 1½ cups of water total. Knead the dough on a work surface until smooth. Cover the dough with an overturned bowl and allow to rest for 30 minutes.

WITH a rolling pin on a lightly floured work surface or using a pasta machine, roll the dough thin, but not as paper thin as you would roll egg pasta. Cut the sheet of dough into strips about ¼-inch wide. Roll each strip under your palms on the work surface to round and thin it. (The pasta should be a little thinner than spaghetti, since it will expand as it cooks.) Dust lightly with flour and set aside.

IN a large skillet, heat 2 tablespoons of the olive oil over medium-high heat. Add the garlic and red pepper flakes. When the garlic becomes fragrant, add the crushed tomatoes and cook for 20 minutes until reduced to a sauce. Season with salt and pepper and remove from the heat.

BRING a large pot of water to a boil, season with the coarse salt (see page 22), and add the pici. Cook until al dente (see page 22). Ladle out ½ cup of the pasta water, then drain the pasta. Add the pasta to the sauce, toss, and cook together over medium heat for 1 minute. Add the pasta water as needed to make the sauce slightly loose and glossy.

PLACE the pasta on warmed plates, drizzle on the remaining 2 tablespoons olive oil, top with the fresh basil, and serve immediately.

MALLOREDDUS ALLA CAMPIDANESE

MALLOREDDUS WITH TOMATO AND SAUSAGE

Serves 4 as a first course

This pasta is made with saffron, which the Phoenicians brought saffron from the Middle East to the island of Sardegna thousands of years ago. It is still used in many local dishes. A little goes a long way, but do use whole threads and not saffron powder. You can also add saffron to the sauce rather than or in addition to incorporating it into the pasta dough. Use a ridged wooden paddle like the one on page 101 to imprint lines into the malloreddus, unless you happen to own a *ciuliri*—one of the wicker baskets used on Sardegna for this purpose.

1 pinch saffron

2½ cups durum semolina flour

1 yellow onion, minced

2 tablespoons extra virgin olive oil

10 ounces fresh sausage

1 cup red wine, preferably Cannonau

2 cups canned peeled tomatoes, chopped

Fine sea salt to taste

Coarse sea salt for pasta cooking water

¾ cup grated Pecorino Sardo

TOAST the saffron in a dry pan until fragrant, then grind to a powder and combine with 1 tablespoon water. Set aside.

ON a work surface or in a bowl, shape the flour into a well. Add ½ cup lukewarm water to the center of the well. Begin to knead, pulling in flour from the sides of the well, and continue until you have a compact, smooth dough. Add a little more water if it feels dry. Sprinkle the saffron water over the dough, then knead briskly to work it in. The dough should be a uniform yellow color. Shape the dough into a ball, cover with an overturned bowl, and set aside to rest for 1 hour.

IN a skillet set over medium heat, sauté the onion in the olive oil until golden. Remove the sausage casing, crumble the sausage, and add it to the skillet. Continue to cook, stirring, until browned. Add the wine and cook until the liquid has evaporated, then add the tomatoes. Season with salt, lower the heat, and simmer, uncovered, until thickened. Remove from the heat.

CUT off a piece of the pasta dough and on a lightly floured work surface roll it into a rope about ¼ inch in diameter. Cut the rope into ¾-inch pieces. Place one piece of dough on a ridged paddle and press with your thumb, rotating it quickly so that the piece of dough both stretches into an oval and curls up on itself. Repeat with remaining dough.

BRING a large pot of water to a boil. Season with coarse salt and cook the pasta until it is al dente (see page 22). While the pasta is cooking, place the grated cheese in a heatproof bowl. Add about 3 tablespoons of the pasta cooking water to the cheese and whisk until melted and smooth. If the mixture seems too thick, add a little more water until it is thin. Drain the pasta and add to the skillet with the tomato sauce. Toss over medium heat, then stir in the cheese mixture and toss to combine. Serve hot.

BUSIATE ALLA TRAPANESE
BUSIATE WITH ALMOND PESTO

Serves 4 to 6 as a first course

Trapani is famous for two things: its picturesque salt pans—which evoke a moonscape and produce exceptionally flavorful sea salt—and its almond pesto. You can keep the pesto at room temperature for a few hours, but no longer.

3¾ cups durum semolina flour

¾ pound (about 2½ cups) cherry tomatoes

1 clove garlic, crushed and peeled

12 large fresh basil leaves

½ teaspoon coarse sea salt, plus more for the pasta cooking water

⅓ cup whole almonds, lightly toasted

½ cup extra virgin olive oil

½ cup grated aged Pecorino Sardo

TO make the pasta, place the flour in a bowl and add about ¾ cup water. Stir with a fork to combine. Continue adding water in small amounts until you have a soft dough. You will probably need between 1 and 1¼ cups of water total. Knead the dough on a work surface until smooth. Cover the dough with an overturned bowl and allow to rest for 30 minutes.

CUT off a piece of dough and roll into a very thin rope—less than ⅒ inch in diameter and thinner than a pencil. Cut the rope into pieces 4 inches long. Place a piece of dough on the work surface and place a skewer on top of it at a 45-degree angle to the piece of dough. Gently roll the skewer toward you while thinning the dough and wrapping it around the skewer so that it forms a corkscrew. (This sounds more complicated than it is. Just be sure not to press too hard or the dough will stick to the skewer and be hard to remove.) Gently slide out the skewer and set aside the corkscrew-shaped pasta. Repeat with remaining dough. Set pasta aside in a single layer and allow it to dry slightly.

IN a mortar and pestle (or blender), crush the tomatoes. Add the garlic and crush thoroughly. Add the basil, ½ teaspoon salt, and almonds. Grind until the mixture is finely broken down. Then continue to grind while adding the olive oil in a steady stream. Taste and adjust the salt.

BRING a large pot of water to a boil, season with coarse salt (see page 22), and cook the pasta until it rises to the surface of the water. Drain the pasta and transfer to a warm serving bowl. Top with the pesto and toss to combine, then sprinkle on the cheese, toss again, and serve immediately.

CAVATELLI CON PISELLI E PROSCIUTTO

CAVATELLI WITH PEAS AND PROSCIUTTO

Serves 4 as a first course

Eggless pasta made with semolina flour is found throughout southern Italy. Cavatelli look like small shells. Their hollows are perfect for trapping peas.

3¾ cups durum semolina flour

Coarse sea salt for cooking water

1 cup fresh shelled peas

3 tablespoons extra virgin olive oil

3 tablespoons unsalted butter

3 ounces prosciutto crudo, diced

1 cup minced shallots

Freshly ground black pepper to taste

Juice of ½ lemon

2 tablespoons chopped fresh flat-leaf parsley

1 cup grated Parmigiano Reggiano

TO make the pasta, place the flour in a bowl and add about ¾ cup water. Stir with a fork to combine. Continue adding water in small amounts until you have a soft dough. You will probably need between 1 and 1¼ cups of water total. Knead the dough on a work surface until smooth. Cover the dough with an overturned bowl and allow to rest for 30 minutes.

PULL off a piece of dough and roll into a thin rope about ¼ inch in diameter on a lightly floured work surface. Cut the rope into 2-inch pieces. Place one piece on the work surface in front of you. Pressing gently in the center with your fingers, push the piece of pasta dough away from you so it thins in the center and the sides curl up. Repeat with remaining dough. Let the shaped pasta dry for about 30 minutes.

PREPARE a bowl of ice water. Bring a large pot of water to a boil and season with coarse salt (see page 22). Blanch the peas in boiling water, then transfer them to the ice water to stop the cooking. Add the pasta to the boiling water and cook until al dente (see page 22).

WHILE the pasta is cooking, heat the olive oil and butter in a large skillet. Add prosciutto and cook until crisp. Add the shallots and sauté until they become translucent. Add the blanched peas and pepper and stir.

RESERVE about 1 cup pasta cooking water, then drain the pasta and add to the skillet with the lemon juice and parsley. Toss to combine, then remove from heat and stir in the Parmigiano Reggiano. If the pasta seems too dry, stir in pasta cooking water about 1 tablespoon at a time. Serve immediately.

CAVATELLI CON RICOTTA E RAPINI

CAVATELLI WITH RICOTTA AND BROCCOLI RABE

Serves 4 to 6 as a first course

This dish pairs chewy semolina flour cavatelli with creamy ricotta and slightly bitter broccoli rabe. Sometimes cavatelli are made with a little ricotta incorporated into the dough. If you'd like, you can try that method instead. Simply force the ricotta through a sieve to make it perfectly smooth and reduce the amount of water you add to the flour to make the dough.

3¾ cups farro flour (see page 129)

6 large ripe tomatoes, or 2 cups tomato puree

Coarse sea salt for pasta cooking water

2 cups tightly packed broccoli rabe

¼ cup extra virgin olive oil

3 ounces prosciutto cotto, diced

Fine sea salt and freshly ground black pepper to taste

¼ cup ricotta

TO make the pasta, follow the instructions on the opposite page, using the farro flour.

MAKE the sauce: If using fresh tomatoes, process them through a food mill. Bring a large pot of water to a boil for cooking the pasta. Season with coarse salt (see page 22), then add the pasta.

MEANWHILE, bring another pot of water to a boil, salt, and blanch the broccoli rabe. Drain and squeeze dry, then chop and set aside. In a skillet, heat 3 tablespoons of the olive oil. Add the tomato puree. Cook for 2 minutes, then stir in the prosciutto cotto and the broccoli rabe. When the cavatelli are cooked al dente (see page 22), remove with a slotted spoon or skimmer and transfer to the skillet, reserving the cooking water. Cook the pasta in the sauce over medium heat, tossing vigorously, for 3 minutes. Stir in a little of the pasta cooking water if the skillet looks dry. Taste and season with salt and pepper. Drizzle with the remaining 1 tablespoon of olive oil.

DISTRIBUTE the pasta among individual serving plates and top each serving with a dollop of the ricotta. Serve immediately.

IL GRANO È CHIAVE

Flour is made by milling a dried ingredient, usually a grain (and most commonly wheat), but sometimes other items as well, such as chestnuts or dried chickpeas. Whole grain flours contain all parts of the kernel: the bran, the germ, and the endosperm. More refined flours have been sifted to remove the germ and bran. Flour also has different grinds. For pasta, you will almost always be using finely ground flour. A more coarsely ground flour will give pasta a gritty taste.

FARINA EINKORN

Like farro (see opposite), einkorn is an ancient strain of wheat. Indeed, einkorn has been grown for more than 10,000 years. Because of its protein structure, it is often a good option for people with gluten sensitivity, though it is not gluten-free.

FARINA DI SEMOLA DI GRANO DURO

Semolina flour is a hard wheat, high-protein flour that makes pasta with a chewy texture. Most dried pasta is made with semolina flour, and many handmade flour-and-water pastas (i.e., eggless), the kind known as maccheroni in the south, are made with semolina flour as well. Look for finely ground semolina flour, sometimes labeled durum flour or durum semolina. It will feel silky and be a pale yellow color.

➤ *Durum is Latin for "hard."*

CHICCHI DI GRANO

FARINA 00

Wheat berries are ground to make whole wheat and all-purpose flours. In Italy we have special traditions associated with the whole berries. Part of Eastertime celebrations throughout the southern regions, pastiera is a torte filled with custard and studded with wheat berries and candied orange. Then there is cuccia, a simple dish of simmered wheat berries stirred with ricotta and honey, which is eaten to mark the feast of Santa Lucia in December but also makes a healthful breakfast any time of the year.

➤ Wheat berries, or grano, carry deep meaning in Italy, symbolizing the fall harvest as well as the rebirth of spring—the cycle of life.

There is a lot of confusion about 00 flour. While in the United States flour is usually categorized by its protein content, or hardness, in Italy it is categorized by grind. 00 flour is very finely ground—it feels like talcum powder. Pasta dough made with 00 flour is very smooth, but unbleached all-purpose flour is a close match.

FARRO

Farro is a specific kind of wheat that dates back many centuries in Italy. Soldiers in the Roman army subsisted largely on a kind of porridge made with farro. Whole farro makes a tasty addition to soups and can be used to make grain salads, but farro finds its groove when it is ground into flour that is used to make pasta. Farro pasta has a nutty flavor and is earthy without tasting heavy.

BIGOLI IN SALSA

WHOLE WHEAT SPAGHETTI WITH ANCHOVIES AND ONIONS

Serves 4 as a first course

Bigoli are a whole wheat handmade pasta similar to extra-thick spaghetti. They can be made with or without eggs. Bigoli are extruded with a special tool that resembles a meat grinder, but a home pasta machine (either electric or hand-cranked) will also work, and instructions for using one are provided below. Making the pasta using either machine is not difficult, but if you prefer, simply replace the bigoli below with a high-quality artisanal whole wheat spaghetti.

3 large yellow onions

⅓ cup extra virgin olive oil, plus more for drizzling

3 cups whole wheat flour, plus more for flouring the pasta

4 large eggs or 1 cup water

8 anchovy fillets, minced

Freshly ground black pepper to taste

Coarse sea salt for pasta cooking water

Fine sea salt to taste

THINLY slice the onions into half-rings.

PLACE the oil in a large pan over low heat. Add the sliced onions, separating the rings as you add them to the pan, and cook, stirring occasionally, until the onions are wilted, about 15 minutes. Do not allow them to brown. Add ⅔ cup water to the pan, cover (use foil if you don't have a tight-fitting lid large enough), and simmer over low heat until the onions have dissolved, about 1 hour. Check the onions occasionally and add a little water to keep them from sticking, if necessary.

WHILE the onions are cooking, make the pasta dough with 3 cups whole wheat flour and the eggs or water through step 4 (finishing the dough and setting it aside to rest) on page 68. When the dough has rested, either process it through a bigoli machine, or roll it out on a crank machine set to the second- or third-thinnest roller setting, whichever is closest in thickness to the width of your most narrow pasta-cutting setting. Let the dough rest until it feels dry to the touch, then roll it through the most narrow notched pasta-cutting rollers on the machine. Toss with a little additional flour to keep the pasta from sticking, spread on a baking sheet or tray, and set aside.

STIR the minced anchovy fillets into the cooked onions and continue to cook, uncovered, until the anchovies have dissolved, about 5 minutes.

BRING a large pot of water to a boil for the pasta. When the water is boiling, salt it (see page 22) and add the pasta. Cook until al dente (see page 22), reserve about 1 cup of the pasta cooking water, and drain the pasta in a colander.

TRANSFER the drained pasta to the pan with the onions and anchovies. Stir in 1 tablespoon at a time of the pasta cooking water to moisten the dish—you will probably need 2 to 4 tablespoons. Toss the pasta vigorously over medium heat until well combined. Taste and adjust salt and season liberally with freshly ground black pepper and a generous drizzle of olive oil. Serve immediately.

PIZZOCCHERI

BUCKWHEAT PASTA WITH CHEESE AND CABBAGE

Serves 4 to 6 as a first course

Buckwheat pizzoccheri from the Valtellina area are baked in a cheesy casserole that is perfect for a chilly winter evening. Look for the local red wine called Sforzato to pair with this dish.

3 cups buckwheat flour

1 cup OO flour or unbleached all-purpose flour

8 tablespoons (1 stick) unsalted butter, plus more for the pan

Coarse sea salt for pasta cooking water

1 large potato, peeled and diced

1 small head Savoy cabbage, cored and chopped

1 small yellow onion, minced

Fine sea salt and freshly ground black pepper to taste

½ cup grated Parmigiano Reggiano or Grana Padano

½ cup shaved fontina cheese

COMBINE the two types of flour and shape into a well in a bowl or on a work surface. Add some water to the center of the well and begin to pull in flour from the sides of the well, adding more water as needed, until you have a crumbly dough. You will probably need between 1 and 1½ cups of water total. Knead until firm and well combined. Cover with an overturned bowl and allow to rest for 30 minutes.

PREHEAT the oven to 400°F. Butter a 9-by-13-inch baking pan and set aside. Roll the dough into a thin sheet and cut into strips about ½ inch by 3 inches.

BRING a large pot of water to a boil, season with coarse salt (see page 22), and add the potato and the cabbage. When the water returns to a boil, gradually add the pasta. Cook until pasta is al dente (see page 22) and potato is tender, 10 to 15 minutes. Meanwhile, melt the butter in a skillet over medium heat and sauté the onion until browned. Drain pasta, potato, and cabbage and transfer to the prepared pan. Pour the butter-and-onion mixture on top, season with salt and pepper, and toss gently to combine. Sprinkle on both types of cheese and toss to combine. Bake until the cheese has melted and the top is dotted with brown spots, about 15 minutes. Let the pasta rest for a few minutes before serving.

PASTA RIPIENA

Eating stuffed pasta is like opening a gift.

PASTA RIPIENA

Stuffed pasta is egg pasta dough rolled thin, dotted with a filling, and then cut into individual pieces that are sealed. Certain types of stuffed pasta, such as tortellini, are then shaped further. Some Italian cooks add a few drops of olive oil or milk to the dough for stuffed pasta, which makes it easier to seal. Dough for stuffed pasta must be rolled thin, as in places it will form a double layer.

Of course, when it comes to pasta, Italian ingenuity knows no bounds. These days you'll see lots of new shapes on menus all over Italy (and at Eataly as well): caramelle are "candies" with the ends twisted to resemble candies wrapped in cellophane, and fagottini or sacchetti are bundles or beggar's purses. Below are some of the classic shapes we make fresh daily at Eataly.

CAPPELLETTI

These "little hats" look like tri-corner hats and are filled with meat and cheese inland and with fish along the Adriatic coast. They are folded into triangles and then formed into rings.

PANSOTTI

These half-moons (or occasionally triangles) from the Italian Riviera in Liguria get their names from their big bellies. The cuisine of Liguria is heavy on greens, and pansotti almost always have some greens in their filling.

AGNOLOTTI DEL PLIN

Agnolotti del plin are Piemonte's signature pasta. A plin is a "pinch" in local dialect, as the way these are sealed is by pinching each piece together.

RAVIOLONI

Big ravioli are beautiful. A large raviolone with an egg inside that releases its yolk when cut is a real showstopper at the dinner table.

➤ *Always have your filling ready before you roll out pasta dough. The dough can dry out if it sits too long. Filling for stuffed pasta should be creamy but dry. It should clump together if you squeeze a piece in your hand. If it's so dry that it's crumbly, moisten it with water or another liquid until it is the right consistency. If it's too loose, add breadcrumbs in small amounts until it feels correct.*

RAVIOLI MAGRI
CHEESE RAVIOLI

Serves 4 as a first course

Magro means "lean" and is used to indicate any meatless dish in Italy. You can serve these meatless ravioli in a butter sauce or a light tomato sauce. You can also incorporate other types of soft or grated cheese in the filling, such as a goat's milk robiola or even mascarpone. Just be sure the filling is smooth but firm enough to hold its shape. You can thin it with a little milk or cream, if necessary.

2 cups ricotta

3 cups 00 flour or unbleached all-purpose flour

3 large eggs

1 cup grated Parmigiano Reggiano or Grana Padano, plus more for serving

Fine sea salt and freshly ground black pepper to taste

Coarse sea salt for pasta cooking water

Butter-Sage Sauce (see page 147)

PLACE the ricotta in a cheesecloth-lined sieve set in a bowl, place a small pot lid on top, and drain for at least 8 hours in the refrigerator.

MAKE a pasta dough with the flour and eggs. (See page 68).

FOR the filling, in a bowl combine the drained ricotta and the 1 cup Parmigiano Reggiano. Season to taste with salt and pepper.

ROLL out the pasta dough. Cut a piece of dough into a strip about 8 inches wide. Gently mark the dough with the back of a butter knife down the center of the strip from short end to short end, marking out two long rectangle shapes. Arrange 1 tablespoon of the filling centered in the middle of one half. (If the strip is long enough, arrange multiple portions on the dough, evenly spaced apart.) Brush the dough around the filling with water. Fold the empty half of the pasta over the filling and press gently around the filling to seal. Cut with a ravioli cutter. Remove scraps and reserve for another use. Continue with the remaining dough and filling. Let the ravioli dry on a lightly floured surface for 1 hour.

WHEN you are ready to cook the ravioli, bring a large pot of water to a boil and season with coarse salt. Add the ravioli and cook, stirring, until they rise to the surface, about 5 minutes. Drain and toss with the butter-sage sauce and serve immediately with additional grated cheese on the side.

How to Make Ravioli

RAVIOLI ARE PROBABLY THE BEST-KNOWN STUFFED PASTA. Indeed, the word "ravioli" is often used as a synonym for stuffed pasta in general. Classic ravioli are square, but there are also round ravioli, sometimes marked as *ravioli tondi*. Examples of round ravioli include the anolini of Parma and Piacenza, which are almost always filled with meat.

Whatever their shape, ravioli can be filled with vegetables, meat, cheese, fish, or almost anything else you can imagine, though they were likely originally filled with rapa, or turnip greens. At least that's one of several theories about the etymology of the word. Other possibilities include the idea that the stuffed pieces of pasta themselves—with their bulging centers—resembled small turnips, and that the word derives from the Genova dialect word *rabiole*, or "worthless stuff," presumably because any leftover bits and pieces could be used up in the filling.

When you consider how far back ravioli date, it's no wonder that it's hard to pin down their origins. There are references to packets of dough with filling as far back as the Middle Ages in Italy, and Giovanni Boccaccio wrote about ravioli in his fourteenth-century masterpiece, *The Decameron*. Even then, Italians knew a good thing when they heard about it. In the scene, one character describes a town where all the residents do is make "macaroni and ravioli" and cook them in capon broth. "Oh," responds a listener, "that must be a wonderful place."

Ravioli filling needs to hit a Goldilocks-style balance: neither too runny nor too dry. It should be perfectly smooth, never chunky, and creamy. A filling that is too liquid will be difficult to handle and leak out of the little packets; a filling that is not soft enough will be unpleasantly pasty once the pasta is cooked. Drained ricotta is an excellent base for a filling and can be supplemented with all kinds of minced or pureed vegetables. Any meat you use in a filling should be ground finely and cooked in advance.

Use two spoons to dollop out the filling in the center of the dough strip.

Place a top layer on top of the filling and press the edges down gently.

Use a stamp, rotelle cutter, or a sharp knife to cut out the ravioli.

Pull away the scraps of dough and reroll to make more ravioli.

MEZZELUNE AI PISELLI
HALF-MOONS WITH PEAS

Serves 4 as a first course

Celebrate late spring with bright sweet peas wrapped in fresh pasta and dressed in a refreshing lemon-butter sauce.

2 cups ricotta

3 cups 00 flour or unbleached all-purpose flour

3 large eggs

2 cups shelled peas

Leaves of 1 bunch fresh mint

1 pinch freshly grated nutmeg

½ cup grated Grana Padano or Parmigiano Reggiano

Fine sea salt and freshly ground black pepper, to taste

Coarse salt for pasta cooking water

5 tablespoons unsalted butter

Zest of 1 lemon in strips

PLACE ricotta in a cheesecloth-lined sieve set in a bowl, place a small pot lid on top, and drain for at least 8 hours in the refrigerator.

MAKE a pasta dough with the flour and eggs. (See page 68).

BRING a pot of water to a boil and prepare a bowl of ice water. Blanch first the peas and then the mint, transferring them to the ice water. Drain the peas and squeeze the mint dry. Place both in a food processor fitted with the metal blade and process until smooth. In a bowl, fold together the drained ricotta, pea mixture, and grated cheese. Season with salt and pepper.

ROLL out the pasta dough. Using a cookie cutter, cut circles with a 3½- to 4-inch diameter from the strips of pasta. Reroll scraps and cut out additional circles.

PLACE about 1 tablespoon of the pea mixture slightly off center on each circle of dough. Fill a small bowl with lukewarm water. Lightly moisten a fingertip and run it around the perimeter of one circle, then fold the circle in half, pressing the edges together to seal. Set aside and repeat with the remaining circles of dough.

WHEN you are ready to cook the mezzelune, bring a large pot of water to a boil and season with coarse salt. (See page 22.) Add the mezzelune and cook, stirring, until they rise to the surface, about 5 minutes. (See page 22.) Meanwhile, in a large skillet melt the butter over medium-low heat. Add the lemon zest and heat gently to release its aroma. When the pasta is cooked, drain and transfer to the skillet with the butter. Toss gently to coat and serve hot.

CASUNZIEI
PASTA STUFFED WITH BEETS

Serves 4 as a first course

Cortina d'Ampezzo in the Veneto region is the Aspen of Italy: a chic mountain town known for great skiing and great food like beet-stuffed casunziei. If you purchase the vacuum-packed cooked beets sold in some Eataly stores, you can skip the messy beet-cooking step.

2 medium beets

2 medium potatoes, preferably not waxy

1 small yellow onion, minced

9 tablespoons (1 stick plus 1 tablespoon) unsalted butter

Fine sea salt and freshly ground black pepper, to taste

3 cups 00 flour or unbleached all-purpose flour

3 large eggs

Coarse salt for pasta cooking water

2 tablespoons poppy seeds

½ cup grated Parmigiano Reggiano or Grana Padano

PLACE the beets in a pot with water to cover, bring to a boil, then simmer until soft enough to pierce with a paring knife. Place potatoes in a separate pot and do the same. Sauté the onion in 1 tablespoon of the butter until golden. When potatoes and beets are cool enough to handle, peel them and puree them together with the cooked onion. Taste and adjust seasoning.

MAKE a pasta dough with the flour and eggs. (See page 68).

ROLL out the pasta dough. Using a cookie cutter, cut circles 2½ inches in diameter. Reroll scraps and cut out additional circles.

PLACE about ½ teaspoon of the beet mixture slightly off center on each circle of dough. Lightly moisten a fingertip and run it around the perimeter of one circle, then fold the circle in half, pressing the edges together to seal. Repeat with remaining dough and filling.

BRING a large pot of water to a boil and season with coarse salt. (See page 22.) Add the casunziei and cook, stirring, until they rise to the surface, about 5 minutes. (See page 22.) Meanwhile, in a large skillet melt the remaining 8 tablespoons butter over medium-low heat. Add the poppy seeds and toast. When the pasta is cooked, remove with a slotted spoon or skimmer and transfer to the skillet. Toss gently to coat and serve hot with grated cheese on the side.

➤ Don't poke potatoes and beets often to test them as they are cooking, as they will become waterlogged.

EATING ON TOP OF THE WORLD

CORTINA D'AMPEZZO IS LOCATED IN the Dolomites, a UNESCO World Heritage Site mountain range that is actually part of the southern Alps. The Dolomites are known for their especially jagged formation and unusual colors, as well as for being a prime location for skiing and other outdoor pursuits.

The Dolomites can feel like a world apart. Natives speak their own language, Ladin, and—this is Italy, after all—have their own cuisine. The local food mixes Italian, Austrian, and Swiss influences and is well-suited to the surrounding micro-climate. In this area, that means there are lots of warming dishes suitable for a cozy night in front of a fire. Indeed, the Dolomites are famous for their many *rifugi*—casual inns where you can ski or hike up to the door, indulge in a fabulous meal, and often spend the night.

In addition to casunziei, in this region you'll find *pestarei* (a kind of milk soup), *faariesa* (another soup made of fava beans and barley), *knödel* dumplings, polenta, and *pastìn* (a kind of meatball that incorporates several different types of meat and a few chunks of savory salami). Game stews are served with a dollop of lingonberry jam on the side, and potatoes play a starring role and are often pan-fried with speck. Cows are pastured in these mountains, and as a result the area produces many highly regarded cheeses. Desserts often look to Austrian traditions and can include apple strudel and Sacher torte, as well as buckwheat cake with a thin layer of jam and lacy *furtaies* fritters. A *bombardino*—warm brandy and eggnog topped with a generous amount of whipped cream—is enjoyed at night and sometimes in the morning as a pick-me-up.

TORTELLI DI ZUCCA
PASTA STUFFED WITH SQUASH

Serves 4 as a first course

Mantova's tortelli or ravioli di zucca are large squares or rectangles filled with winter squash sweetened with crushed amaretti cookies. Sometimes mostarda—a chutney-like local specialty—is in the mix. Ferrara's cappellacci di zucca are very similar but don't include amaretti. They are sometimes served in Bolognese ragù for an interesting sweet-and-savory contrast.

1¼ pounds butternut squash

4 cups 00 flour or unbleached all-purpose flour

4 large eggs

4 ounces amaretti cookies, crumbled

1¼ cups grated Parmigiano Reggiano or Grana Padano, plus more for serving

1 tablespoon grated lemon zest

Fine sea salt to taste

Butter-Sage Sauce (see opposite) made with 8 tablespoons (1 stick) butter and 8 fresh sage leaves

PREHEAT the oven to 400°F. Halve and seed the squash and cut into large slices. Bake until soft, about 30 minutes. Remove the squash from the oven and let it cool. Once it is cool, scrape the flesh of the squash off the rind and wrap it in a kitchen towel, place the towel in a colander, and let it drain for 10 minutes.

MEANWHILE, make a pasta dough with the flour and eggs. (See page 68).

COMBINE the amaretti cookies, grated cheese, and lemon zest. Add the drained squash and a pinch of salt and stir until smooth and fully combined.

ROLL out the pasta dough into a thin sheet. Arrange 1-tablespoon portions of filling about 2 inches apart in rows on one side of the sheet of dough. Brush the dough with water between the filling. Fold the empty side of the sheet over the filling, press gently with your fingers to seal, then cut rectangles out of it around the mounds of filling. Be certain to seal the edges of the pasta.

BRING a large pot of water to a boil. Season with coarse salt. Cook the ravioli until they rise to the surface. Drain and toss with the butter-sage sauce to coat, then serve hot passing cheese on the side.

SALSA CLASSICA: BUTTER-SAGE SAUCE

BECAUSE FILLED PASTA IS COMPLEX, you don't embellish it much. Small filled pasta often floats in broth (see pages 73, 154, and 163). Larger stuffed pasta is instead most frequently glossed simply with butter. While melted butter is plenty tasty and works well to highlight the bright flavors of spring, as in our mezzelune ai piselli on page 143, browning the butter that you will serve over pasta (and crisping a few sage leaves in the butter) adds nutty, toasty flavor. Browning butter simply means cooking the proteins in the butter until they darken slightly.

Browning butter isn't difficult or time-consuming, but you can't plunk the butter on the stove and walk away. Place unsalted butter in a light-colored pot (so you can monitor the color). Place over medium-low heat and melt the butter, breaking it into pieces and stirring occasionally with a heatproof spatula. When the butter has melted, add fresh sage leaves.

Now the water begins to evaporate. Swirl the pot frequently, and guard against spatters. Every once in a while scrape the bottom and sides of the pot with the spatula. Otherwise flecks of protein may stick and begin to color faster than the rest. The sage will begin to crisp.

Once the butter begins to foam, stir constantly. You can brown the butter as dark as you like—anywhere from pale golden to rich mahogany. If necessary, spoon out a little butter onto a white dish to assess the color. You can also judge by smell. Just be sure to pull the butter off the heat before it turns dark or acrid.

Immediately transfer the butter and sage to a heatproof bowl to cool, stirring it occasionally to move along the process. You can pour the butter and sage over cooked pasta and toss to combine, or toss the pasta with the butter and sage in a skillet very briefly, stirring in a little pasta cooking water if needed. A sprinkling of grated cheese always pairs well with butter and sage.

This butter-sage sauce will keep for a week or so in the refrigerator.

PANSOTTI CON SALSA DI NOCI
PANSOTTI IN WALNUT SAUCE

Serves 4 as a first course

Pansotti (the Ligurian dialect word for "belly," sometimes spelled *pansòti* or *pansòtti*) are half-moon or triangular ravioli filled with greens and ricotta that are traditionally served in a walnut sauce. We also like to serve them with a simple sauce of melted butter and lemon zest with a handful of pistachios scattered on top. If the ricotta you purchase (or make) for your pansotti filling has a large quantity of liquid, drain it in a fine-mesh strainer for an hour or so. You want it to be fairly dry, so that when you pinch a bit of the filling and roll it between your fingertips it forms a ball.

8 ounces spinach

¾ cup ricotta, drained if necessary

1 cup plus 2 tablespoons grated grana cheese (see page 87), plus more for serving

2 teaspoons fine sea salt

Pasta dough made with approximately 3 cups unbleached all-purpose flour and 3 large eggs, cut into strips 3½ to 4 inches wide (see page 68)

2 cups walnuts

2 cloves garlic

6 tablespoons extra virgin olive oil

3 tablespoons chopped fresh flat-leaf parsley

Freshly ground black pepper to taste

Coarse sea salt for pasta cooking water

3 tablespoons unsalted butter, cut into pieces

COOK spinach as described on page 90, squeeze as dry as possible, and mince by hand. Combine the spinach, ricotta, ¾ cup grated cheese, and 1 teaspoon salt and mix to combine. Taste and adjust the salt.

USING a cookie cutter (we use a fluted cutter at Eataly, which is pretty, but ravioli with a plain border will taste just as good) or the rim of a juice glass, stamp out circles with a 3½- to 4-inch diameter from the strips of pasta. Reroll scraps and cut out additional circles. (You will always end up with a few odd scraps of dough, but we usually roll those last few scraps into rough circles and use them anyway.)

PLACE about 1 tablespoon of the cheese and spinach mixture slightly off center on each circle of dough. Fill a small bowl with lukewarm water. Lightly moisten a fingertip and run it around the perimeter of one circle, then fold the circle in half, pressing the edges together to seal. Set aside and repeat with the remaining circles of dough.

WHEN all the pasta is ready, make the sauce. Toast the walnuts either in a dry skillet or in a 350°F oven or toaster oven until fragrant, about 5 minutes in the skillet and 8 to 10 minutes in the oven or toaster oven.

WITH a mortar and pestle or a food processor fitted with the metal blade, process the walnuts and the garlic until they are finely chopped but not ground into a powder. With a spatula, scrape the nut and garlic mixture into a bowl. Stir in the olive oil, 6 tablespoons of the grated cheese, the parsley, and 1 teaspoon salt until thoroughly blended. Taste and season with pepper and additional salt if needed.

BRING a large pot of water to a boil for the pasta. When the water is boiling, season with coarse salt (see page 22) and add the pasta. Cook until the pasta rises to the surface of the water, probably no more than 3 minutes (see page 22).

USE a strainer to scoop the pasta out of the cooking water and into a warmed serving bowl; reserve about 1 cup cooking water. Scatter the butter on top of the pasta and toss to melt the butter and to combine. If the walnut sauce seems thick, thin it with a few tablespoons of the pasta cooking water, then add the walnut sauce to the pasta and toss to combine. Again, if the sauce is chunky and doesn't adhere to the pasta, add a little of the pasta cooking water, about 1 tablespoon at a time, until the pasta is nicely coated. Serve immediately with additional grated cheese on the side.

RAVIOLONI ALL'UOVO E TARTUFO
LARGE EGG RAVIOLI WITH TRUFFLE

Serves 6 as a first course

This dish offers both olfactory and visual drama: the rich aroma of black truffle, and the golden yolk that bursts out when you cut into a single-portion raviolo. You can use either sheep's milk or cow's milk ricotta—just be sure to use the full-fat version. You will use only the yolks of the eggs, but they must remain intact. Reserve the whites for another use.

8 ounces spinach

½ cup ricotta, drained if necessary

2 tablespoons heavy cream

½ cup grated Parmigiano Reggiano

Pinch freshly grated nutmeg

Fine sea salt and freshly ground black pepper, to taste

Pasta dough made with approximately 4 cups 00 flour or unbleached all-purpose flour and 4 large eggs (see page 68)

6 large eggs

1 stick (8 tablespoons) unsalted butter

Coarse sea salt for pasta cooking water

Black truffle for shavings

STEAM the spinach as described on page 90. Squeeze dry and mince finely. You should have about ½ cup. In a bowl, combine the ricotta, cream, ½ cup grated Parmigiano Reggiano, and nutmeg. Season with salt and pepper and fold in the spinach.

ROLL out the pasta dough. Cut it into two strips of the same width but with one piece of dough 1½ inches longer than the other. Place the shorter strip of dough on the work surface. Arrange the filling in 6 equal mounds with equal distance between them. Make a well in the center of each mound of ricotta. Separate 1 egg and carefully transfer the intact yolk to the center of one of the ricotta mounds. Repeat with remaining yolks.

PLACE the second sheet of pasta gently over the mounds and carefully press the dough with your fingers to seal the ravioli. Do not let air pockets form. Using a large cutter or knife, cut into ravioli. Arrange in a single layer on baking sheets lined with lightly floured kitchen hand towels and cover with additional towels.

WHEN you are ready to cook the pasta, bring a shallow pot of water to a boil and season with coarse salt. Melt the butter in a skillet. Add 1 cup boiling water to the skillet with the butter, stir, and simmer until the liquid reduces by half, about 2 minutes. Stir in the remaining ¼ cup grated Parmigiano Reggiano and warm over very low heat.

TURN down the water to a gentle boil and with a wide slotted spatula gently lower 1 raviolo into the gently boiling water. Cook for 2 minutes. Gently lift out the raviolo and set aside. Repeat with remaining ravioli. Transfer the cooked ravioli to the skillet with the butter sauce, egg-side up, and cook for 1 additional minute, using a spoon to gently baste the ravioli with the sauce. Transfer to individual serving dishes and shave truffle over the top. Serve immediately.

How to Shape Tortellini and Cappelletti

TORTELLINI AND CAPPELLETTI ARE VERY SIMILAR. The only real difference in shape is that tortellini begin with a circular piece of pasta that is stuffed and folded into a half-moon, and cappelletti begin with a square that is folded into a triangle. (As for filling, tortellini always contain at least some pork, while cappelletti fillings can vary. A debate rages about size—some people will tell you that tortellini are always slightly larger than cappelletti, while others insist the inverse is true.) Both are then wrapped around a finger for a final shaping.

Such stuffed pieces of dough first appeared at banquets in Italy in the Middle Ages, when well-to-do families in Bologna feasted on tortellorum on special occasions. Obviously, the manual labor involved in creating small pieces of pasta was intense, so serving tortellini and cappelletti was a sign of wealth and power.

Making tortellini and cappelletti is still a labor of love today, but in areas where these pastas are signature dishes, no holiday would be complete without them. In Italy, children are often recruited to do the folding and shaping—their narrow fingers are perfect for wrapping and sealing smaller rings. You can prepare the filling for tortellini and cappelletti up to several days in advance. Filled and shaped tortellini and cappelletti also freeze beautifully. Simply arrange them in a single layer on a tray and freeze, then transfer to freezer bags. You can drop them into boiling water or broth directly from the freezer without defrosting them—they may take a minute or two longer to cook.

Roll out your egg pasta dough and cut it into squares or circles. Place filling in the center of several of the pieces. Moisten the edge of the pasta with a finger (it's helpful to keep a small bowl of water on the work surface next to you) and fold the square into a triangle (or fold a circle into a semi-circle).

Press with your finger along the edge to seal. This is important, as you don't want filling to leak out while the pasta is cooking.

Pick up a sealed triangle and wrap it around a finger so the two points overlap slightly. (Or do the same with a semi-circle.) Press to seal.

Flip down the top point (or round edge on tortellini) so that the piece resembles a tri-corner hat. Set aside on a lightly floured surface to dry while you finish the rest.

➤ Roll out one egg-size piece of pasta dough at a time and leave the rest covered or wrapped to prevent them from drying out.

Fold the square into a triangle, pinching the edges.

Wrap the shape around your forefinger.

Pinch the circle to close it and pull the top point out.

TORTELLINI IN BRODO

TORTELLINI IN BROTH

Serves 8 to 10 as a first course

Tortellini are little circles that are folded and formed into rings. Legend has it that the shape was created as an homage to the belly button of Venus, as glimpsed through a keyhole by an innkeeper. Purchase prosciutto and mortadella in a chunk (not sliced) to make the filling. You can replace up to half of the pork with veal or a combination of veal and turkey, but pork is always the hallmark of tortellini. Tortellini that have already been stuffed and shaped freeze nicely. Spread them out in a single layer on a pan in the freezer for about 45 minutes, then once they're frozen, toss them into a zippered storage bag. They can go right from the freezer into the cooking water or broth without thawing. For the broth, use any beef cuts suitable for long cooking—shank, ribs, and so on. Traditionally, a capon is used in the broth, but you can replace the capon with turkey or with some additional beef. This recipe is a bit of a project, but each component (with the exception of the pasta dough) can be made in advance.

2 pounds beef on the bone

2 pounds capon

2 ribs celery, chopped

2 carrots, chopped

1 large yellow onion, peeled and chopped

1 bay leaf

1 sprig fresh flat-leaf parsley

2 cloves garlic

1 tablespoon whole black peppercorns

2 tablespoons unsalted butter

COMBINE the beef and capon in a large stockpot. Add enough water to cover by about 4 inches and bring to a boil. Skim off any foam and add the celery, carrots, onion, bay leaf, parsley, garlic, and peppercorns. Bring to a boil, then reduce the heat to a simmer and cook at a low simmer, partially covered, for 3 hours. Strain the broth into a large bowl (save the meat for another use) and let it cool, then refrigerate until the fat hardens on the surface. Remove almost all of the fat (leave about 1 teaspoon behind for flavor) and discard. Refrigerate the broth until you're ready to use.

MELT the butter in a large skillet over medium heat. Add the pork and sage leaves and cook over medium heat until the meat begins to brown, then reduce the heat to low and cook until the pork is cooked through, about 15 minutes more. Remove and discard the sage. Allow to cool slightly.

8 ounces pork loin, chopped

2 fresh sage leaves

4 ounces prosciutto crudo

4 ounces mortadella

½ cup grated Parmigiano Reggiano

Pinch freshly grated nutmeg

Fine sea salt to taste

Freshly ground black pepper to taste

1 large egg, lightly beaten

Pasta dough made with approximately 3 cups unbleached all-purpose flour and 3 large eggs (see page 68)

IN a food processor fitted with the metal blade or a meat grinder, grind the cooked pork and its juices with the prosciutto and mortadella, then add the cheese and nutmeg. The mixture should form a ball when you grab a bit with your hand, but it should still have a bit of texture to it. Season with salt and pepper. Mix in the egg and set the filling aside to cool, or refrigerate for up to 8 hours.

ROLL a portion of pasta dough into a very thin sheet (see pages 70–71 for specific instruction). Leave the remaining dough covered. Arrange the sheet of pasta dough on a work surface. Use a cookie cutter to cut out disks of pasta dough about 1½ to 2 inches in diameter, as close together as possible. Save the scraps and reroll them, or cut them into small squares and serve them in soup. (You can freeze them in a zippered storage bag.)

PUT about ¼ teaspoon of the filling on one of the disks. Fold in half to form a semicircle, pressing to seal. (If the pasta is dry and the edges won't stick together, brush the edges with a little water.) Press the two ends of the flat side of the semicircle together around your index finger to form a ring. The flat side should fold up to form a kind of cuff. Seal the two ends together, overlapping them slightly. Repeat with the remaining dough and filling.

PLACE the broth in a large pot and bring to a boil. Salt the broth and taste to be sure it is properly seasoned. Add the tortellini a few at a time. About 1 minute after they rise to the surface (this should happen fairly quickly, in about 3 minutes or less; see page 22), remove them with a slotted spoon and transfer to soup bowls. Ladle broth over the cooked tortellini and serve.

CAPPELLETTI DI PESCE

FISH CAPPELLETTI

Serves 6 as a first course

Along the Adriatic coastline, cappelletti are filled with fish. These can either be served in a broth made with the bones of the fish you used in the filling or in a simple fresh tomato sauce. (If you are not serving the pasta in broth, you can start with fillets rather than a whole fish. Cook with the shallot and puree the mixture together.) Gurnard and turbot are good choices for the filling, but any white fish will do. Just skip the oily species.

1 (2-pound) whole fish, scaled and gutted

1 rib celery

1 carrot

1 onion

1 clove garlic

½ cup white wine

3 sprigs fresh flat-leaf parsley

1 small shallot, minced

1 tablespoon extra virgin olive oil

Fine sea salt and freshly ground black pepper to taste

¼ cup heavy cream

Pasta dough made with approximately 4 large eggs and 4 cups 00 flour or unbleached all-purpose flour, rolled and cut into 2-inch squares (see page 68)

Coarse salt to taste

IN a stockpot, combine the fish, celery, carrot, onion, garlic, wine, and parsley. Add enough water to cover the fish by about 2 inches. Bring to a boil, then simmer until the flesh of the fish is opaque and flaky, about 15 minutes. Remove the fish and bone and skin it. Return the bones to the pot and continue cooking until you have a flavorful broth, 15 to 30 additional minutes. Strain broth and set aside.

MEANWHILE, sauté the shallot in the olive oil until softened. Mince the cooked fish and shallot together. Season with salt and pepper. Stir in cream a little at a time until you have a smooth filling that is firm enough to clump together when you pinch off a piece, but not dry or crumbly. Set aside.

PLACE ¼ teaspoon of the fish filling on one square of pasta dough. Fold, seal, and shape. (See page 152.) Repeat with remaining dough squares and filling.

STRAIN the broth, bring to a boil, season, and cook the ravioli in the broth just until they float to the surface, 3 to 4 minutes. Taste and adjust seasoning and serve hot.

HOW TO SERVE PASTA

MAKING PASTA IS MORE THAN JUST COOKING—it's part of a ritual handed down for centuries. Unlike many foods, pasta cannot be cooked in advance. With very few exceptions, it must be cooked just before serving and served warm. Some sauces can be prepared in advance, and baked dishes like lasagne can be assembled in advance and even baked and then reheated before serving, but for the most part, you're going to have to boil a pot of water, salt it, and cook the pasta in the half hour or so before you plan to eat.

The good news is that none of those tasks are difficult. In summer, we love all kinds of uncooked sauces—think chopped fresh tomatoes or pesto. Some pasta needs nothing more than a little brown butter and sage and a sprinkling of cheese (see page 147). Stuffed pastas like those in this chapter are already little individual flavor bombs. A complex sauce would overwhelm them or compete with them.

Pasta asciutta (meaning "pasta in a sauce," i.e., not soup) is traditionally served "family style" in a low, wide serving bowl, although there are some pastas that are best portioned into individual bowls at the stove. Always warm your serving bowl before using. Simply fill it with hot water, slosh the water around for 30 seconds or so, then spill it out into the sink. Using a warm bowl makes a difference. You can warm individual serving bowls as well. Individual servings of pasta asciutta are always presented in low, wide soup bowls—never on flat plates or in deep cups.

Short pasta can be scooped out with a large serving spoon. Long pasta can be lifted out of the serving bowl with a large fork and spoon. Don't forget to run your spoon around the bottom of the bowl to collect any bits that have gathered down there and distribute them among the individual serving bowls. Soup, of course, can be portioned out with a ladle. If you are serving grated cheese on the pasta, it's best to pass a cheese grater with small holes and a hunk of cheese and allow people to grate it onto their own portions. The amount of cheese a person likes—or doesn't—is highly personal.

At Eataly, we talk a lot about seasonal ingredients, but eating seasonally is about more than simply using the vegetables that are growing at any given moment. It's also about shaping menus that are suitable to the weather. That means lighter foods in summer, and heartier and richer dishes in winter. The genius of Mother Nature is that if you eat seasonally, this will happen naturally on its own.

AGNOLOTTI DEL PLIN CON BURRO FUSO

AGNOLOTTI DEL PLIN IN MELTED BUTTER

Serves 4 as a first course

The pride of Piemonte, agnolotti del plin are little squares of meat-filled pasta like miniature ravioli that are served in a butter sauce or the juices from roasted meat. They are typical of the region's cuisine: luxurious, yet lacking in artifice. *Plin* is dialect for "pinch," which refers to the way these are sealed. If you prefer, you can cut the pasta into squares first and then fill each square with the meat mixture; we think the method described below is a little quicker and easier.

8 ounces spinach

5 tablespoons unsalted butter

1 small yellow onion, minced

1 clove garlic, thinly sliced

1 pound ground beef or veal or a combination of the two

Fine sea salt to taste

½ cup grated Grana Padano cheese (see page 87)

Pinch freshly grated nutmeg

Pasta dough made with approximately 3 cups unbleached all-purpose flour and 3 large eggs, cut into strips 1 inch wide (see page 68)

Coarse sea salt for pasta cooking water

4 fresh sage leaves, minced

STEAM the spinach as described on page 90. Squeeze dry and set aside.

MELT 1 tablespoon butter in a large skillet over medium heat. Add the onion and cook, stirring frequently, until the onion is translucent, about 5 minutes. Add the garlic and cook until it begins to brown, about 5 minutes more. Add the meat to the pan, crumbling it in with a fork. Brown the meat. Season the mixture with salt and remove from the heat; let cool slightly.

MINCE the meat mixture and the spinach together. (Do this by hand—a food processor or blender will make it mushy.) Stir in the grated cheese and the nutmeg.

ARRANGE one strip of pasta dough on a work surface. Place ¼ teaspoon of the meat mixture 1 inch apart down one long side of the strip. Fold the other (empty) half of the strip over the side with filling. With your fingers, gently press between the small mounds of filling to seal the two halves together. With a serrated pastry wheel, trim the long (unfolded side) of the dough, then cut between the small mounds of filling with the pastry wheel. You should have 1-by-½-inch agnolotti. Repeat with the remaining dough and filling.

BRING a large pot of water to a boil. When the water is boiling, season with coarse salt (see page 22) and add the pasta. Cook until the pasta rises to the surface of the water (see page 22), probably no more than 3 minutes.

MEANWHILE, heat the remaining 4 tablespoons butter in a saucepan large enough to hold the pasta over very low heat. Remove from the heat as soon as the butter is melted.

DRAIN the pasta and add the pasta to the pan with the butter. Toss to coat the pasta. Stir in the minced sage. Divide equally among 4 heated pasta bowls and serve immediately.

AGNOLOTTI VERDI
GREEN AGNOLOTTI

Serves 6 as a first course

Piemonte and Liguria border each other, and these agnolotti—the signature pasta of the former—filled with borage—a common ingredient in the latter—are made along that border. Borage is a light and slightly lemony green. If you can't locate it, you can also use spinach or chard in the filling.

2 cups tightly packed borage

3 tablespoons unsalted butter

2 leeks, thinly sliced

½ cup grated Grana Padano cheese (see page 87), plus more for serving

Fine sea salt to taste

Spinach pasta dough made with approximately 4 cups flour, 1 pound spinach, and 4 large eggs, cut into strips 1 inch wide (see page 68)

Coarse sea salt for pasta cooking water

Butter-Sage Sauce (see page 147)

BRING a pot of water to a boil and blanch the borage. Squeeze dry and chop. Melt the butter in a small skillet and sauté the leeks and cooked borage. Mince the mixture together with the ½ cup grated cheese and season to taste with salt.

ARRANGE one strip of pasta dough on a work surface. Place ¼ teaspoons of the borage mixture 1 inch apart down the left side of the strip. Fold the right (empty) half of the strip over the left. Brush the dough with water. With your fingers, gently press between the small mounds of filling to seal the two halves together. With a serrated pastry wheel, trim the long (unfolded side) of the dough, then cut between the small mounds of filling with the pastry wheel. You should have 1 inch by ½ inch agnolotti. Repeat with remaining dough and filling.

BRING a large pot of water to a boil for the pasta. When the water is boiling, season with coarse salt (see page 22) and add the pasta. Cook until the pasta rises to the surface of the water, probably no more than 3 minutes. Remove pasta with a spoon or slotted skimmer, toss with the butter-sage sauce, and serve hot with additional grated cheese on the side.

PLAY WITH YOUR FOOD

OKAY, DON'T ACTUALLY PLAY WITH YOUR FOOD—that would be bad manners. But you can manipulate fresh pasta in several interesting ways.

For green pasta: Rinse spinach and steam in the water that clings to the leaves. Chop it as finely as you can. Add it to the flour well with the eggs in step 1 and proceed. The pasta dough may need a little extra flour to balance out the moisture the spinach provides. Use about ¼ pound of fresh spinach per egg/portion. Most common shapes: lasagne, tagliatelle. Serve with meat sauces, such as the ragù on page 48, or stuff with a cheese filling for vegetarian pasta. You can also combine egg and spinach tagliatelle for *paglia e fieno*, or straw and hay—delicious with a sauce of peas and cubes of prosciutto.

For black pasta: Add squid ink to the flour well with the eggs in step 1 and proceed. Use about 1 tablespoon squid ink per egg/portion. Most common shapes include tagliatelle and tagliolini. Serve with any seafood sauce.

For striped pasta: Make a batch of dough and leave three-fourths of the dough plain egg pasta and flavor the other fourth with spinach or squid ink. Roll out both types of dough. Place the plain sheet of dough on a work surface. Roll out the green or black dough and cut into strips. Place the strips evenly on top of the plain dough and roll again to seal them together. Even if it looks a little wonky at this point, once you cut and shape and cook it, no one will notice. We particularly like to use striped pasta for *caramelle*: stuffed pasta tubes with twisted ends that resemble hard candies in wrappers.

CAPPELLETTI IN BRODO AL POMODORO

CAPPELLETTI IN TOMATO BROTH

Serves 4 as a first course

Don't be fooled by the familiarity of the ingredients here—this is a very sophisticated dish. The tomato broth concentrates the flavor of fresh tomatoes.

1 bunch fresh basil

5 pounds plum tomatoes

1 tablespoon fine sea salt, plus more to taste

2 ice cubes

2 cups ricotta

Grated zest of 3 lemons

½ cup freshly grated Grana Padano cheese (see page 87)

Freshly ground black pepper to taste

Pasta dough made with 4 large eggs and 4 cups 00 flour or unbleached all-purpose flour, rolled and cut into 3-inch squares

Coarse salt for pasta cooking water

12 cherry tomatoes, halved

SET aside a few basil leaves for garnish. To make the broth, puree the tomatoes, basil, the 1 tablespoon fine sea salt, and ice cubes in a blender until smooth. Strain through a cheesecloth-lined sieve set over a bowl to drain at room temperature for at least 8 hours. Place the ricotta in another cheesecloth-lined sieve set in a bowl, place a small pot lid on top, and drain in the refrigerator for at least 8 hours.

FOLD the lemon zest and grated grana into the drained ricotta. Season to taste with salt and pepper and stir until all ingredients are thoroughly incorporated.

PLACE ½ teaspoon of the ricotta filling on one square of pasta dough. Fold, seal, and shape. (See page 152.) Repeat with remaining dough squares and filling. Arrange the cappelletti in a single layer on a baking sheet sprinkled with flour and let them dry for a hour.

BRING a large pot of water to a boil, season with coarse salt, and cook the pasta al dente. Drain and divide among individual serving bowls. Meanwhile, gently heat the tomato liquid in a medium saucepan. Pour the heated tomato broth over the pasta. Garnish with reserved basil and the cherry tomatoes and serve immediately.

TORTELLINI CON PANNA E PROSCIUTTO

TORTELLINI WITH CREAM AND PROSCIUTTO

Serves 6 as a first course

Tortellini are frequently served in broth, as on page 154, but if you want to enjoy them in the form of *pasta asciutta*, or pasta with a sauce rather than in soup, they can be covered with a simple cream sauce. This is also tasty with peas or sliced mushrooms added to the sauce.

2 tablespoons unsalted butter

½ cup diced prosciutto cotto

2 cups heavy cream

1 pinch freshly grated nutmeg

Fine sea salt and freshly ground black pepper to taste

Coarse sea salt for pasta cooking water

1 batch tortellini (page 152)

½ cup grated Parmigiano Reggiano or Grana Padano

MELT the butter in a large skillet over medium heat, add the prosciutto and cook, stirring, for 30 seconds to combine. (Don't brown the prosciutto.) Add the cream and stir to combine. Season with nutmeg and salt and pepper. Simmer gently to reduce while you cook the pasta.

BRING a large pot of water to a boil and season with coarse salt. (See page 22.) Add the tortellini and cook until they rise to the surface. (See page 22.) Remove the tortellini with a slotted spoon or skimmer and add to the skillet with the cream. Toss briefly off heat to combine. Serve hot with grated cheese on the side.

➤ Prosciutto cotto is cooked rather than cured like prosciutto crudo.

CANNELLONI DI CARNE

CANNELLONI WITH MEAT

Serves 6 to 8 as a first course

The ricotta for cannelloni should be on the dry side so that liquid doesn't leak out into the pan while the pasta is baking; drain in a cheesecloth-lined sieve if necessary.

2 yellow onions, minced

2 tablespoons extra virgin olive oil, plus more for oiling pan

1 pound ground beef

¼ cup red wine

Fine sea salt to taste

1 (16-ounce) can whole peeled tomatoes

1 pinch freshly grated nutmeg

2 cups ricotta

1 egg, lightly beaten

1½ cups grated Grana Padano cheese (see page 87)

Besciamella made with 3 tablespoons unsalted butter, ¼ cup flour, and 2 cups milk, reduced to the consistency of sour cream (see page 111)

Coarse sea salt for pasta cooking water

About 18 fresh 4-by-4-inch egg pasta strips made with approximately 2 cups unbleached all-purpose flour and 2 large eggs (see page 68)

IN a pot, sauté the onions in the olive oil until softened. Add ground meat and cook, breaking it up with a fork, until it is no longer red. (Do not brown.) With a slotted spoon, transfer about half the meat to a bowl and allow to cool. Add wine to the pot and cook until the liquid has evaporated. Season with salt and add the canned tomatoes and juices. Simmer over low heat until thickened, about 45 minutes. Meanwhile, season the cooked beef in the bowl with salt and nutmeg and stir in the ricotta, the beaten egg, and about 1¼ cups of the grated cheese. The mixture should be creamy but firm. If it feels too dry, stir in a little of the besciamella.

PREHEAT the oven to 400°F. Bring a large pot of water to a boil. Spread a kitchen towel on a work surface and set a bowl of ice water nearby. When water boils, season with coarse salt and add 4 of the pasta squares. Cook until the pasta rises to the surface, about 30 seconds, then remove with tongs, dip briefly in the cold water, and spread on the dish towel in a single layer. Repeat with remaining squares. Gently blot dry. Oil a 13-by-9-inch baking dish.

SPOON about ⅓ cup of the ricotta mixture along the edge of one of the pasta squares, leaving a ½-inch margin. Roll into a tube and place in the prepared baking dish, seam side down. Repeat with remaining pasta and filling, tucking them next to each other. Cover with the tomato sauce, then pour the besciamella on top of that. Sprinkle on remaining grated cheese. Bake until golden and bubbling, about 15 minutes. Let stand 5 to 10 minutes before serving.

Pasta Ripiena Alla Grande

When we say *pasta ripiena*, or stuffed pasta, we think mostly of ravioli and tortellini, but there is another type of stuffed pasta in Italy: larger-size pieces of pasta that are cooked, filled, and baked. These include cannelloni, lumaconi or conchiglioni (large shells), and the like. Some of these dishes can be made with dried semolina pasta or with fresh pasta, though you will break our *cuori Piemontesi* (hearts) if you even suggest creating our beloved cannelloni with dried pasta. Baked stuffed pasta is great for a crowd.

The pasta is always cooked first before baking. Prepare a bowl of ice water and a baking sheet lined with clean kitchen towels. Follow the instructions on page 22 to cook pasta in a generous amount of boiling water seasoned with coarse sea salt. When the pasta is al dente, use tongs to dip it briefly in the ice water, then transfer to the towel-lined pan in a single layer. Gently blot the pasta dry with another towel.

Fill the pasta with a smooth filling—almost always there is ricotta involved, though the possibilities are virtually endless. A spoon is fine for this—the pasta will be covered partially by a sauce—but if you are a real neatnik you can use a pastry tube to fill the pasta.

Arrange the pasta in a lightly oiled or buttered baking dish. The pasta should fit companionably in a single layer without being smushed together so that the filling oozes out and without being so far apart that it unfurls or opens up.

Top the pasta with a sauce. Without sauce it will dry out too much in the oven.

Sprinkle grated cheese in an even layer on top of the pasta. Some types of pasta are also dotted with butter.

Bake in a preheated oven until the pasta is heated through and the cheese has browned into a golden crust. It is always a good idea to let baked pasta settle for 5 to 10 minutes before serving.

Use a large spoon to gently fill each cooked pasta shell.

Top with sauce before baking to keep the pasta from drying out too much.

FAGOTTINI DI RICOTTA CON MELANZANE E POMODORO

RICOTTA BUNDLES WITH EGGPLANT AND TOMATO SAUCE

Serves 8

Be sure to roll the pasta for this dish fairly thin, as the squares will be doubled up. These bundles are beautiful as is, but if you really want to make an impression you can tie them around the top with chives or blanched strips of leek. If you don't have enough ramekins, a muffin tin will work.

1 pound plum tomatoes

About 5 tablespoons extra virgin olive oil

Fine sea salt and freshly ground black pepper to taste

2 sprigs fresh thyme

4 medium eggplants (about 6 pounds total)

1 (16-ounce) can whole peeled tomatoes

1 tablespoon red wine vinegar

2 cups loosely packed fresh basil leaves

1¼ cups grated Grana Padano cheese (see page 87)

Coarse sea salt for pasta cooking water

About 32 fresh 6-by-6-inch egg pasta squares made with approximately 3 cups unbleached all-purpose flour and 3 large eggs (see page 68)

3 cups ricotta, drained in a cheesecloth-lined sieve if very liquid

Freshly ground white pepper to taste

1 large egg, beaten

PREHEAT the oven to 400°F. Line 2 large baking sheets with foil and set aside.

CUT the plum tomatoes in half lengthwise and toss with 1 tablespoon of the olive oil. Season with salt and pepper. Place the thyme sprigs on one of the lined baking sheets and arrange the tomatoes on the sheet, cut side down. Place the eggplants (whole) on the second baking sheet and roast both until the tomato skins turn dark and puff and the eggplant skin looks dark and tears easily and the eggplant pulp is completely tender, about 15 minutes. (Tomato and eggplant may be done at different times.) Cool both slightly, remove the skins and seeds from the eggplants. and chop the roasted tomatoes and eggplant coarsely. Leave the oven on.

PLACE the roasted tomatoes and eggplant in a large saucepan. Lift the canned tomatoes out of their juices and crush them by hand into the pot. Cook over medium heat for 5 minutes, then add red wine vinegar and adjust salt to taste. Continue cooking until the mixture tastes homogenous, about 5 additional minutes. Tear in the basil and stir in 2 tablespoons of the grated grana.

MEANWHILE, bring a large pot of water to a boil for cooking the pasta. Spread a clean flat-weave kitchen towel on a work surface and set a bowl of ice water nearby. When the water is boiling, salt it with the coarse salt and add 4 of the pasta squares. Cook until the pasta rises to the surface, about 30 seconds, then remove with a skimmer, dip briefly in the cold water, and spread them on the towel in a single layer. Repeat with remaining squares. Gently blot the squares dry.

COMBINE the ricotta and 1 cup of the grated grana in a bowl. Season to taste with salt and white pepper. Stir in the egg.

BRUSH 16 medium ramekins with some of the olive oil and place them on a baking sheet. Lightly brush a flat plate with oil and place one square of pasta on it. Brush the top of the pasta square with oil. Place about ¾ cup of the ricotta filling in the center and place another square of pasta on top at an angle so that the two squares together resemble an 8-pointed star. Gently lift the two squares of pasta and fit them into one of the ramekins with the corners standing up vertically. Repeat with remaining pasta and filling. Spoon eggplant and tomato sauce over the bundles (reserve any leftover sauce) and sprinkle with the remaining 2 tablespoons grana. Bake in the preheated oven until browned, about 20 minutes. Let stand 5 minutes before unmolding. Gently reheat any leftover tomato and eggplant sauce and serve it with the bundles.

CRESPELLE AL FORMAGGIO
CHEESE CRESPELLE

Serves 4 to 6 as a first course

Versatile *crespelle*—Italian crepes—can be filled any number of ways. In Abruzzo, crespelle are also sprinkled with grated aged cheese, rolled into tubes, and served in a shallow pool of hot broth. Almost any of the region's dozens of cow's milk, goat's milk, and sheep's milk cheeses will work in this filling.

1 cup whole milk

2 large eggs

2 tablespoons melted butter

Fine sea salt to taste

¾ cup 00 or unbleached all-purpose flour

½ cup chopped walnuts

1 cup fresh caprino

1 cup grated scamorza cheese

1 cup grated aged Pecorino cheese

¼ cup minced chives

Extra virgin olive oil for oiling pan and baking dish

WHISK together the milk and eggs. Whisk in the melted butter. Add a pinch of salt and gradually sprinkle in the flour while whisking constantly. Strain any lumps. Let batter rest, covered, for at least 1 hour and up to 8 hours. (Refrigerate if resting for longer than an hour.)

TOAST the walnuts until fragrant. Combine the walnuts, the caprino, the scamorza, and about half of the aged pecorino with the chives. Season to taste and set aside.

PREHEAT the oven to 400°F. Lightly oil a skillet and place over medium heat. Add a small amount of batter, about 2 tablespoons for an 8-inch skillet, and swirl to coat the surface thinly. Cook until brown around the edges, then flip, and cook the other side. (It will cook very quickly.) Repeat with remaining batter, oiling the pan again when necessary.

OIL a baking dish. Fill each of the crespelle with a little of the cheese and walnut filling and roll into a tight cylinder. Tuck the rolled crespelle in the prepared baking dish, seam sides down. Sprinkle on the remaining ½ cup grated aged pecorino and bake in the oven until browned and heated through, about 10 minutes. Serve warm.

➤ Caprino is goat's milk cheese. The name comes from *capra*, or "goat."

INDEX

CONVERSION TABLES

LIQUID CONVERSIONS	
U.S.	Metric
1 tsp	5 ml
1 tbs	15 ml
¼ cup	60 ml
⅓ cup	75 ml
⅓ cup + 2 tbs	100 ml
½ cup	120 ml
¾ cup	180 ml
¾ cup + 2 tbs	200 ml
1 cup	240 ml
1 cup + 2 tbs	275 ml
1¼ cups	300 ml
1⅓ cups	325 ml
1½ cups	350 ml
1¾ cups	400 ml
1¾ cups + 2 tbs	450 ml
2 cups (1 pint)	475 ml
2½ cups	600 ml
4 cups (1 quart)	945 ml (1,000 ml is 1 liter)

WEIGHT CONVERSIONS	
U.S./U.K.	Metric
½ oz	14 g
1 oz	28 g
1½ oz	43 g
2 oz	57 g
2½ oz	71 g
3 oz	85 g
3½ oz	100 g
4 oz	113 g
5 oz	142 g
6 oz	170 g
7 oz	200 g
8 oz	227 g
9 oz	255 g
10 oz	284 g
11 oz	312 g
12 oz	340 g
13 oz	368 g
14 oz	400 g
15 oz	425 g
1 lb	454 g

OVEN TEMPERATURES		
°F	°C	Gas Mark
250	120	½
275	140	1
300	150	2
325	165	3
350	180	4
375	190	5
400	200	6
425	220	7
450	230	8
475	240	9
500	260	10
550	290	Broil

GRAZIE INFINITE

to Dino Borri and Sarah Dowling for supervising the editorial production of this book at every stage, as well as to Fitz Fallon, Tom Bohan, Michael Nogera, Luca Montersino, Jason Neve, Samuel De Los Santos, Eli Anderson, Keith Stodola, Matthew Smith, Denis Dello Stritto, Cristina Villa, Lara Beggin, Stacy Stout, Alexa Kennedy, Caitlin Addlesperger, and Sara Massarotto.

First published in the United States of America in 2018 by Rizzoli International Publications, Inc.
300 Park Avenue South
New York, NY 10010
www.rizzoliusa.com

© 2018 Eataly, Inc.

Text by Natalie Danford
Photographs by Francesco Sapienza,
FrancescoSapienza.com
Development and project editor: Christopher Steighner
Production editor: Tricia Levi
Design by Vertigo Design NYC

2018 2019 2020 2021 / 10 9 8 7 6 5 4 3 2 1

Distributed in the U.S. trade by Random House, New York
Printed in China
ISBN: 978-0-8478-6300-6
Library of Congress Control Number: 2018943335

WHAT SHAPE ARE YOU FEELING?

Choose the shape that best matches your taste and your sauce . . .

SIMPLICITY

SPAGHETTI

Spaghetti look like pieces of string, or spago. Since early forks weren't sharp and had only three tines, they weren't good for eating pasta. So spaghetti started out as finger food. Spaghetti was particularly popular because it was easy to pick up by hand.

EXPLOSION

VESUVIO

This is a twisted form of pasta that looks like Mount Vesuvius. Excellent with vegetable-based sauces.

INFINITY

CASARECCE

A piece of this curled pasta looks like a rolled-up parchment scroll. Casarecce resemble handmade pasta and match beautifully with a classic Neapolitan meat sauce.

DEPTH

RIGATONI

Rigatoni were originally produced only for central Italy and especially Roma. Classic rigatoni romani are paired with pajata, or calf intestines.

CONTINUITY

CALAMARATA

The name of this pasta derives from its resemblance to the sliced bodies of squid. It matches well with seafood in dishes such as calamarata, or calamari pasta tossed with actual calamari.

CURIOSITY

ZITI

In the old days, unmarried women—zite—stayed home on Sundays to cook pasta rather than attending mass. This pasta was named for them.

ENERGY

PACCHERI

Pacchero is Neapolitan dialect for "slap." The sound of this pasta being mixed with sauce is said to sound like someone being hit.

IMPERFECTION

ORECCHIETTE

This pasta has noble Medieval origins. It was introduced in Puglia by the Angevin dynasty, which ruled southern Italy in the thirteenth century.

INVENTION

ELICHE

These spirals, or helixes, are larger than classic fusilli. They are perfect for capturing sauce.